I0419908

TRANSITION OF THE MIND

THE JOURNEY FROM HOODLUM TO SAINT:
A CONFLICT OF TWO NATURES

TONY CLOUD, PHD

WestBow
PRESS
A DIVISION OF THOMAS NELSON

Copyright © 2013 Tony Cloud, PhD.

All rights reserved. No part of this book may be used or reproduced by
any means, graphic, electronic, or mechanical, including photocopying,
recording, taping or by any information storage retrieval system
without the written permission of the publisher except in the case
of brief quotations embodied in critical articles and reviews.

WestBow Press books may be ordered through booksellers or by contacting:

WestBow Press
A Division of Thomas Nelson
1663 Liberty Drive
Bloomington, IN 47403
www.westbowpress.com
1 (866) 928-1240

Because of the dynamic nature of the Internet, any web addresses or
links contained in this book may have changed since publication and
may no longer be valid. The views expressed in this work are solely those
of the author and do not necessarily reflect the views of the publisher,
and the publisher hereby disclaims any responsibility for them.

Any people depicted in stock imagery provided by Thinkstock are
models, and such images are being used for illustrative purposes only.
Certain stock imagery © Thinkstock.

Scripture taken from the King James Version of the Bible.

ISBN: 978-1-4908-1079-9 (sc)
ISBN: 978-1-4908-1080-5 (e)

Printed in the United States of America.

WestBow Press rev. date: 12/11/2013

TABLE OF CONTENTS

ACKNOWLEDGMENTS

First of all I would like to thank God for bringing me through the good, bad and ugly days of my life and for having the patience allowing me to go on. I thank Him for giving me the ability to complete the writing of this book.

I extend my sincerest gratitude to my family and friends for their love, commitment, help, dedication continual prayers and support.

I would like to offer my special thanks to Dr. Jim Benton, PH.D, who provided me with very valuable insights, challenges and encouragement.

This book is dedicated to my lovely wife Nikki who stands beside me and believes in me. Her creative genius has been my inspiration and has helped me on this incredible journey with strength giving me the motivation to succeed.

I thank my wonderful teenage children D'Angelo and Tierra who have such understanding hearts and a great love for God. Your continual laughter, love and smiles have been a blessing from God to us all.

PREFACE

Violence in the world has existed from the beginning. Violence itself stems from the tremendous moral and spiritual decline of humanity. When human beings devalue life, nothing remains sacred. Violence is not limited to poverty or increased by riches; it simply exists on every level and in every corner of the world. America has been one of the wealthiest nations that have ever existed from the days of humanity. In spite of that known fact, violence exists in every state of the union. As morality continues to decay, Americans will continue to suffer from detestable violence on every level. Gang violence in particular has escalated in the past seventy years and has gotten out of control. From the great effects of slavery, the "Great Depression," segregation and racial-prejudice violence have become a regular part of our society.

In addition to gang violence and hatred, there is America's drug and alcohol crisis. Drugs and alcohol are usually connected to gang violence or violence in some way. The dilemma has reached deep into the hearts of children at a very young age. Gone are the days when adults committed major crimes and children petty crimes. Now citizens of all ages have joined the societal crisis. It does not end there. Drugs and violence have affected the hearts of the entire world. They have plagued the minds of those who have an opportunity for success and those who have no hope. We must take action now before it is eternally too late.

Most agree that something needs to be done. I submit to you that a transition of the mind must occur for success. An inward desire to change is but the beginning. An environmental change of both mind and location bring a greater opportunity for success. This change brings a different point of view of life through exposure. Exposure helps to eradicate a mind of hate and violent aggression.

My hope is to help save the next generation. I desire to open the eyes of adults so that we can see the tremendous burden that we have placed on the children of tomorrow.

This research and literature have come from a combination of personal experiences, interviews of inner-city adults, and literature developed and written by many different artists, who through music, poetry, and books have reached out to society through their creative talents.

CHAPTER 1

ASPIRING TO JOIN A GANG

I was raised in a violent city and personally indulged in the lust of the eyes, lust of the flesh, and boastful pride of life. I, like many others, have done things that I am not proud of in any way.

For many years, Washington DC and its metropolitan area have held the reputation of being the crime capital of the world. According to a government study, "A Black man in DC who turned 18 in 1989 had a 1 in 24 chance of being murdered by 1995—the worst odds in the country."[1]

Much of this violence in urban areas carried over from drug problems. Crack was a tremendous problem, because it is highly addictive and it quickly brings in easy money. Crack houses and Crack Cocaine was almost everywhere. In addition to her current struggles, Crack brought a new struggle to the streets of America.

> Between 1984 and 1990, a crack epidemic affected the United States. This epidemic included a surge in number of crack houses, cocaine use and addiction, arrests for cocaine related crimes, murder and robbery, and homelessness, especially in major cities such as New York, Baltimore, Miami, Houston, and Chicago.[2]

---

1   Washington D.C. retains title: Murder capital of the world
    www.prisoncensorship.info/archive/etext/dc/DCmurder.htm...
    MIM Notes 162, May 15, 1998 by a MIM comrade.

2   Societal Evolution-For Better or For Worse
    Monday, June 1, 2009
    Crack Epidemic
    http://merkwerk-1964-1989.blogspot.com/2009/06/crack-epidemic.html

In 1987 I graduated from Wheaton High School which is located in Maryland, so I grew up during this tremendous epidemic. Upon completion of high school, I joined the US Army, and after serving 3 years, I moved to South Central Los Angeles. I have seen and heard many ungodly and incredibly unruly things. Some of what I will discuss involves issues that, in my opinion, small children would not understand and should never see with their young, pure eyes.

The inner city is filled with great conflicts, persecution and struggles within and without. Some of these difficulties are so devastating, mesmerizing and powerful that they have brought each of its victims to their knees. Perhaps because of the widespread existence of crime and the large influence of evil, people here never really question the existence of God as residents of other areas do. The complexities of violent crimes that exist in the inner city are innumerable. Inner-city children exposed to so many adult evils have their minds overwhelmed; an internal struggle of a bewildered mind begins. Hence, the axiom, "You can take the boy out of the hood, but you can't take the hood out of the boy." The present violent conditions force children who have not reached a level of maturity to make uninformed decisions. These children are forced to grow up far too fast and to make many decisions that will affect them for the rest of their lives.

In these neighborhoods, there is confusion between good and evil, right and wrong. Children who witness violent crimes against themselves, relatives, or friends, whether it is child neglect, sexual abuse, other abuse, police brutality, or even hate crimes, realize quickly that things aren't the way that they seem. If the children thought that protection came from family and the laws of the land, they quickly realize the flaw of this teaching. These neighborhoods are very aggressive, fast-paced, and violent. In this place, protection comes from the thugs across the street and not the police. Therefore, violence, when it is for your protection, seems to be good and right—even the violence that was necessary to protect your neighborhood.

Children learn that violence is either going to help them or hurt them. Eventually, they get tired of being hurt by it, so they join the violent aggressors to get their help. When they are tired of being mistreated by others, they join groups or gangs for their protection. They learn quickly to befriend the neighborhood thugs, who are seen in a different light. The negative word *thug* becomes a positive in the child's vocabulary. The very person that society calls a ruthless thug is the one who protects the child when he or she needs it most. The thug does not seem so bad to an adolescent growing up in such a violent society, in spite of what others say.

Now comes the proverbial saying "Don't judge a man until you have walked a mile in his shoes."

These children have grown up witnessing the good and the bad committed by fellow members of their hood. Although some of these children are judged by the world as evil, they are real people trying to stay alive, and most of them have the hope of one day getting out of the hood and making a better life for themselves. They see this man whom society calls a thug as one who cares for them, who laughs and smiles with them, and who loves them. The children show him great respect. The children watched the "thug" defend the neighborhood and keep the bad people out. The children could not understand as they watched the police hunt the man down like an animal. The children knew him by name and learned to respect him, one of the greatest needs of every human being. Then this man is murdered in cold blood—an injustice done. Vindictive violence rules the day in this world because one murder, immoral act or crime sown reaps retribution by the victim's closest friends or family with memories that last a lifetime. Someone has to pay! Like the Hatfields and the McCoys, the battle goes on.

What are these young children to think? How is it possible for these young children to gain a true perspective of life when what they have seen has registered into their minds as an injustice? How can these children ever trust the people who are supposed to protect and serve? Being children, they do not know the truth of what happened. They can only judge the scene by what their young eyes saw. The fact of the matter is that their "father" is now gone.

Contrary to popular belief, inner-city children do not grow up aspiring to join gangs. Although treated as if they have some kind of plague, they are the same little, adorable children with unadulterated minds as you see in all children throughout the world.

As I matured, I asked, "What makes one person's human psyche different from another's?" Is it not the education and the exposure that we receive? We learn in many ways, and survival is always a top priority because of the law of self-preservation. We learn from and through our environment. We learn by what we see and by our inward, instinctual ability to reason.

So what then is the difference between one child and another? The difference is exposure; their families and friends expose the minds of the children to different community events, schools, and beliefs. It has never been intellect or ability that is the difference, because all human minds function in the same way.

CHAPTER 2

BELIEVING A LIE

Have you ever believed something to be true and later, to your disappointment, discovered that it was a lie? It has happened to us all. In fact, most of us must admit that we have been on both sides of that experience; believing a lie and telling lies. No one likes being told a lie. Thus, we all agree that honesty is still the best policy.

What happens when the general population misunderstands or misinterprets the facts or refuses to assess the situation properly? They get a distorted view and draw false conclusions. The premises are distorted or incorrect and consistently lead to false conclusions. One might use the word *prejudice* when referring to the general population. Prejudice? Yes! People prejudge other people, places, and things before they truly uncover all of the facts. People decide if they are going to like foods by the way they look or smell. People decide their activities based on what they are most comfortable doing. If something forces us to move into or toward an uncomfortable position, we rebel. When in contact with strange cultures, places, and people, our comfort zone shrinks, and we react to gain our much-needed space, acceptance, and approval.

The children in chapter 1 whose father was gunned down by the police now develop a form of prejudice in their hearts. Remember that they saw this man in a different light and from another point of view. Their view of thugs, gangs, police, and justice has been challenged, leaving them unbalanced in their minds; they have a distorted view. In short, they now begin to believe the lie as if it were true.

They begin at this early age to stereotype people. All police are bad, and all thugs are good. The police will not protect you, but the gangs will. The police have become an enemy in their minds. It seems to work in reverse for the police. They see all thugs as bad and view them as enemies. It is a terrible misunderstanding and distorted view of humanity. There is good and bad in everything and inside everyone. Yet without a proper conclusion, these children remain obligated to avenge their father's death. The police, however, seem to be more concerned about their brotherhood. Now both sides have drawn false conclusions with distorted views, which give rise to a great deal of unnecessary violence.

Once the seed of hate has been sown into hearts, humanity knows what comes next: war! There are two sides to every war, as there are two sides to every coin. Which side are you on? Which side am I on? Is my heart open and willing to learn, or am I hard-hearted and willfully ignorant? Are human beings ignorant by choice? In my opinion, in many ways, I am afraid that some are—at least in America.

At some point in time, humans must break this horrible cycle of life.

I personally have known of many thugs and gangbangers who were potentially great people, laying a good street foundation into the hearts and minds of these young people. They actually attempted to stir the young people away from the streets and encouraged them to get an education. The thug might believe that he has no chance in society, but in his heart wants the next generation to go in another direction. Yet because of prejudice, stereotypes, and the war on the streets, there are very few opportunities for those on the outside looking in to understand. Likewise, there are good police officers just trying to do their jobs. Both want the same thing at the end of the day: to return home safely to their families.

There are good and bad people in every lifestyle, but one must become blind in order to see. I have heard the saying "Never judge a book by its cover," but to refrain from judging is easier said than done. The world has been deceived and tricked into believing a lie. Stereotypes[3] have been the downfall of humanity. Our parents teach

---

3   Stereotypes are destroying the world because they have led to many false conclusions. From a logical perspective, whenever the premises are false, the conclusion is false. False conclusions prove to be destructive. False conclusions cloud and clutter the minds of humanity. A preconceived idea may be true or false. Morals and principles of life hinge on these ideas. If the idea is false, then the moral will become immoral. Stereotypes lead us to lies, injustice, and profiling. They stand in the way of progress.

us by their examples and their own weaknesses to stereotype. They are disguised[4] in our churches. Stereotyping is witnessed on the streets. It is upheld by our judicial system. A person dresses in a certain way, and by their appearance, they shall be judged. Pimps, priests, businessmen, thugs, prostitutes—you will know them by the way they dress, not by what is in their hearts. Mistaken identity occurs from the seeds of stereotyping and prejudice.

If adults cannot see the harm in stereotyping, why would anyone expect a child to have the wisdom to know better? Adults struggle with the same dilemma of stereotyping. Adults grow up believing these lies about human beings, and these views warp their minds regarding some things. One person has become another's enemy without the knowledge of who that other person is, without the knowledge of anything about the other. He or she simply judged them because he or she could. Is there not something wrong with this type of thinking? This extreme has become an evident reality, and sadly, it seems as though thugs and police will be enemies forever. Stereotyping extends to territories, races, and colors. As crime and hatred increases, stereotyping follows the flow of evil.

Stereotypes make the heart sad, angry, and vengeful. Stereotyping and profiling have driven people to do things that they had no intention of doing. I have seen people steal who had more than enough money and the ability to purchase the item that they have stolen. Why would an individual steal if he or she does not need to? Let us look at a present-day scenario that I, as well as most African Americans, experience on a regular basis. A minority person walks into a store, and most eyes, security, and cameras are on him or her. There are plenty of other people in the store, but we have been targeted. We have no intention to steal, but because we are so offended, we retaliate by doing the very thing of which the company's employees have nonverbally accused us. When people stereotype individuals, treating them as criminals when they have done no wrong, an angry vengeful spirit erupts. No one likes being accused of something that he or she has not done, much less

---

4   Prejudice is disguised in churches because some churches preach one God and one people, but act contrary. These churches were leaders of hate but claimed to be followers of God. They preached unity but practiced segregation. They demanded to be heard but would not speak up. America disguises stereotypes through affirmative action. Stereotyping is disguised because, though it is engrained in the heart, it is unspoken.

being accused of something that has never come into his or her mind. "Innocent until proven guilty" seems to be nothing more than mere words. This attitude is found in relationships, where people argue and fight because of accusations. I know of people who were unfaithful to their mates only because they were tired of being accused of some things that were not true. People can easily relate to accusations and stereotypes in relationships with the opposite sex; should people not be able to relate to problems involving race, color, and territory?

There is a grave danger in believing the lies of today. Those lies surround themselves with stereotypes, generalizations, and profiling.

Dr. Martin Luther King was quoted as saying, "I have a dream that my four little children will one day live in a nation where they will not be judged by the color of their skin but by the content of their character."[5] If people could train their own minds and stop poisoning the minds of their children, the world would be a much better place. The lie often occurs when people generalize and categorize. It proves ignorant when people include others whom they have never met into their generalizations and categories.

Let us not leave this chapter believing that being the victim of stereotyping justifies any illegal activity. All illegal activity is wrong and cannot be justified. My desire is only to challenge humans to take a closer look into the minds of others, to see as they see and to feel as they feel, with the hope that humanity can understand each other better and learn to get along.

---

5   The Huffington Post, January 17, 2011, http://www.huffingtonpost.com/2011/01/17/i-have-a-dream-speech-text_n_809993.html.

CHAPTER 3

THE CODE

When a person thinks of secret societies or organizations, they usually know that there is some kind of secret code. The Masons and the Boy Scouts of America have secret handshakes. There are secret signs, tattoos, and encrypted codes hidden to represent important messages. Graffiti is a code for marking territories, but also for alerting residents of police activity. Prisoners of war in concentration camps used many codes to communicate. The public uses codes every day in common speech. For example, if a person wants to get someone's attention, he or she might clear his or her throat or use a hand gesture. Some codes are used in a system of rules and others as a message.

Now living in a world with computers in this information age, additional codes are necessary. Shorthand uses a series of codes, and cellular phone texting is similar to shorthand. People use codes in all lifestyles. On the streets and among organized crime, there are secret codes. Some street codes, I assume, would not be wise to reveal.

Even professional organizations like the police and the military use codes. Codes have proven to be a very useful tool to communicate messages that need to be concealed from others, or to prove an individual's legitimacy. Codes can be as simple as a text or as sophisticated as the International Morse Code, which has its own alphabet. One might almost say that codes are a secret language unto themselves.

As a child, I can remember learning a code that has stuck with me for life. "What you see here, what you hear here, and what you know about this place stays in this place." Other times I heard, "Don't put our business out there on the streets." That simply means to a child, "Keep your mouth shut." Children might also hear someone say to them, "Don't be a tattletale." As children grow to become teenagers and young adults, that tattletale code translates to, "Don't be a snitch; never rat someone out." Perhaps you too have heard codes similar to these.

Yet these series of codes have proven to be dangerous and detrimental to civilization. In my opinion, they have damaged the social order in so many ways. Instead of people holding fast to their own integrity, they are now given a reason to lie. Instead of providing protection, these codes have allowed countless thousands or maybe even millions to get away with criminal activity that should have brought a conviction. This is where I would like to focus our attention.

If people who have been subjected to the code witness a crime in their communities, on their jobs, at school, or in their homes, whom do they tell? The code suggests that they tell no one. Follow this sad scenario: a young girl is being abused by her stepfather, uncle, or cousin, and as a result is impregnated. She tells her mother, but her mother too is governed by the code. They say nothing to anyone else. They immediately look for an alternative answer other than going to the police. You see, the code of silence is critically dangerous. Oftentimes in these situations, another family member takes the newly born child and raises it as her own. The child grows up in the family, but not until later in his or her life, if ever, does he or she find out who his or her biological parents are.

On the other hand, the sexually abused child being tormented by immoral actions suffers psychologically. Abused children grow up frustrated, fragile, emotionally damaged, and at times physically damaged for life. Often, abused children use sex as their outlet and indulge in promiscuity. Here is a possible answer to the amount of teenage pregnancy in our world. Though we cannot attribute all teenage pregnancy to abuse, it does have its place.

The destructive, negative code sown into these children's minds has caused many children to grow up with hurtful and destructive principles. These issues remain deep inside, hidden in the mind and suppressed because there is no one to tell. There are multitudes of parents who know that their children are being abused. However, because the parents have been abused themselves, they do not say a word. Instead, they place the blame on the child refusing to take action.

To whom can the child go for help? In recent years, many have been discovering that boys belonging to the Roman Catholic religion have been abused by its leaders. To whom could they have gone for help? The following appeared in the Dallas Moring News.

> DALLAS (AP). An international movement of Roman Catholic priests out of countries where they have been accused of abusing children has continued even after the abuse scandal that swept the U.S. church in 2002, the Dallas Morning News found in a year-long investigation.
>
> Hundreds of priests accused of abuse have been moved from country to country, allowing them to start new lives in unsuspecting communities and continue working in church ministries, the newspaper reported in Sunday editions.
>
> The priests lead parishes, teach and continue to work in settings that bring them into contact with children despite church claims to the contrary, the newspaper said. Vatican officials declined to comment Friday after an overview of the investigation was featured on National Public Radio.
>
> In one case, Rev. Frank Klep, a convicted child molester who has admitted abusing one boy and is wanted on more charges in Australia, was placed in Apia, Samoa, in the South Pacific. Australia has no extradition treaty with Samoa.
>
> Klep told the newspaper that neither he nor the church feels an obligation to tell anyone about his past. Few, if any, locals are aware of his history.[6]

This problem applies to all manners of life. One person covers up for another, and justice vanishes. Even the Bible says in Ecclesiastes 5:8: "If thou seest the oppression of the poor, and the violent taking away of justice and righteousness in a province, marvel not at the

---

6   Times Daily - Jun 19, 2004
    "Hundreds of priests shuffled worldwide, despite abuse allegations," June 19, 2004.
    http://news.google.com/newspapers?nid=1842&dat=20040619&id=plUeAAA
    AIBAJ&sjid=YMgEAAAAIBAJ&pg=2358,2638068

matter: for one higher than the high regardeth; and there are higher than they." Some in the world today are taught to suppress knowledge for the safety or benefit of others. This suppression of knowledge has proven to be to the detriment of human life. The truth has been substituted with lies, and honesty has become a product of shame. Whom does this child tell? The shamefulness of this is that it reaches into all aspects of life, known as corruption and injustice. Edmund Burke hit the nail on the head when he said, "All that is necessary for the triumph of evil is that good men do nothing."[7]

The damage done by this code runs down into a bottomless pit of injustice. Children are forced to choose sides at an early age. Whom can they trust? Who really cares? Is it the police or their neighbors? If a child sees or hears of a crime or injustice committed by a neighbor, the police, or Child Protective Services, who can this innocent child trust? Some children become lost and hopeless; some choose gangs, and others choose crime. Oftentimes depending on how hurt or skeptical this child is, these feelings will determine how far into the negative he or she will go.

I wonder about this seed of skepticism that has been sown into the human heart. What would happen to most of the world of crime if people would just stand up for what is right? What if injustices were not found in the courts, and everyone truly received a fair trial in a court of law? I optimistically believe that crime would shrink. If portions of the justice system were not controlled by money or popularity and the guilty person did not get away with crime because of his or her bank account, because of the people he or she knew, or the color of his or her skin, I optimistically believe that people would change their respect for the law. If the code disappeared and honesty and truth prevailed, the innocent would be the protected and the guilty prosecuted. Will that day ever come? Society must demand the protection of the innocent, listen to its children, and reward them for taking a stand. All of humanity is hereby called to the task of living up to the morals and values that are righteous.

Perhaps this is why many African Americans do not reach out for help. Perhaps the code has been so engrained into the mind that people do not think anyone cares enough to help. Can humanity get

---

7   www.quotationspage.com/quotes/Edmund_Burke/.

the help that it truly needs? Will all people learn to treat others fairly and without contempt?

In conclusion, here is the dangerous part: when people see no better way, they hang onto what they know and believe to be true—their roots, whether right, wrong, or indifferent.

> "To him therefore that knoweth to do good, and doeth it not, to him it is sin" (James 4:17).

CHAPTER 4

A FATHERLESS SOCIETY

Good fathers are needed in every home. Anyone can be a sperm donor, but to be a good father takes energy, time, commitment, and a great effort. Strong men are needed, strong fathers who are willing to be counted. Society needs men who are ready to raise children of their own and who are diligently willing to care for them. Society needs fathers who are good husbands to their wives and good uncles to their nieces and nephews. The world is looking for a few good men who will make a difference and take a stand. Are there any men who are up to the task?

Where are the fathers in these young children's lives? The absentee father introduces another problem into this world in which we live: underage children having babies. There are so many young women having babies way before they are ready. The boys, who obviously mature later, as new fathers are in a worse position. They are children ages thirteen and up and even sometimes younger having babies. Imagine being a father or mother at such a young age. Who will care for this newborn child—and how? Where are the parents of these children who are now new parents themselves? It is not only an epidemic; we are in a crisis. It is an issue of morality. Moral decay has entered deep into the recesses of the heart of America.

Unfortunately, instead of men, these are young, immature boys who father babies, boys who are too ashamed of the ridicule that exists for virgins. There is an amazing peer pressure from both sexes against a person's virginity, even though they know that kids should not be sexually active for many great reasons. In the inner city, boys who are virgins are treated as less than males and with extreme contempt. Without the respect of this young man's peers, the social order and status that he one day hoped for becomes a hopeless journey. In the hood and urban societies, not money or fame but respect rules the day. Most will do just about anything to earn it.

Without the respect of the males in the community, the females follow in the same type of taunting mockery against males and females who are virgins, making their lives very undesirable and increasing the level of their personal inner frustrations. The children's hearts and emotions become hardened for a short stint, and they decide to rid themselves of this self-inflicted pain of maintaining their virginity. Young men find a willing young woman and have sex, forgetting the consequences of their actions for just one night. However, with sex outside of a proper loving marriage, there is always a risk, and in time, a tremendous price to pay. I can remember the haunting phrase, "I am pregnant," echoed to many young boys by the girls who helped rid them of their virginity. The initial response was usually, "It's not mine." Denial is a sure indication that they were never ready and certainly immature to say the least.

The unwanted or unclaimed child grows up without a father and replaces the absent father in time with another father figurehead or role model. Unfortunately, there are not many positive role models in the streets. A father figurehead is nothing more than a dominant male on the streets with a reputation. He too most likely grew up without a father in his life. Many fathers from the urban cities are in prisons, dead, or just simply nonexistent. This figurehead could be a drug dealer, gang leader, thug, or just simply ruthless. He could also be a good, upstanding citizen. Either way, he has great respect on the streets. He is not called father and he certainly is an unwilling participant in that area; he is simply a leader. The streets show no partiality and will take these children any way they can get them.

The streets tend to encourage helplessness and hopelessness. Imagine a young man being in a world or a situation that, in his own mind's view, shows no way out. The business world despises him because of the way that he dresses. His hairstyles, though expressive in his neighborhood, become a stench to his possible employer. His slang is not acceptable to society. The young man's parents cannot afford to send him to college. His school is rundown. The teachers are not paid enough to care. He is not looking for pity—he just wants a fair chance—but he does not know the right people nor have the necessary skills yet. The critical area is that either the world does not care about these people or it does not know that they exist. Some know but just do not care. All of this negativity is stacked up against the young mind. However, there is a dim light at the end of the tunnel. There is a way to function and to make money in this world inside of America. The father figurehead makes the young man an amazing deal and a sure way to make money: drugs. In comparison to the above stated issues, the proposition does not sound so bad. He has heard that success and happiness are the American dream. Now the young man can buy those Kix (shoes), jewelry, cars, clothing, and more. He can now experience his understanding of the American dream and the ultimate prize: he gains respect and money, which bring many girls into his life. A young man once discouraged is now on a willful path of destruction because of the hopelessness that he once felt from the pressures of society. Being a father proves that he is not a virgin, and his level of respect has increased that much more.

The young man believes there is a long future in leadership ahead of him. Like good investing, the younger that children begin their journey on the streets, the better chance they have of rising to the top in their community. There is an established pecking order inside of each urban community. In the inner city, a hierarchical pecking order is established in the neighborhood through play and "being down" (ready to do whatever it takes). The more willing the child is, the higher he or she will climb to become a future inner-city leader. This destructive teaching and way of life has to be stopped. Society can contribute to stopping this by offering great jobs and a place for children to go, bringing new skills to its inner-city youths. By instilling hope, the community can greatly discourage these children from the streets. With the lack of adequate funding and so much opposition, these programs, which create opportunity and hope, become unsupported and quickly die out. Every child dreams of success, but success is not always determined by skill in America. Much success apparently comes from whom a person knows and by the opportunities that those acquaintances can present. Rarely do those opportunities exist for children in the hood or urban cities. This is a sad reality but true. A strong father could have kept this young man from this plight.

Why are strong moral fathers so important in the home? A strong father can keep his child from most violence. A strong male figure in the home means protection and stability. Fathers with strong, solid morals are important because they too have a past. Their past reputation earned them great respect in the hood or urban city, and for this reason, their children will be respected and protected. It is almost like an inheritance. Respect on the streets is truly better than money.

CHAPTER 5

DEATH WITHOUT A WEAPON

The power of a mother's love is undeniably important. When her love is missing, the balance of life becomes twisted. There is a bond created from the day of conception. As the embryo grows inside of the womb, the bond grows stronger and stronger. Daily the child hears the sweet sound of Momma's voice clinging to every breath that she or he takes. The womb is a safe haven and a playground—nine complete months of growing, bonding, and feasting. As the infant reaches full term, knowledge of the mom is complete. The child knows his or her mother's voice and smell, and longs for her gentle touch.

Even nature demonstrates the tender care and necessity of a loving mother. In nature, the lioness protects her cubs unto the death. She searches for them when they are missing, frantically calling. She nurtures, educates, plays with, and feeds her cubs. Some of society's unfit mothers would do themselves well to mimic creatures known as unreasoning animals. I know that this sounds degrading, but some have earned this negative thought.

The day of delivery will come, and who knows what awaits this newborn child? What fate does this child face? Will there be love or hate, drugs or sobriety? Will the child have to grow up breathing his or her mother's polluted air from cigarette smoke? What will the child see? Will the child be subject to watching Mom's many failed relationships? Will Mom's frustration be taken out on this child? Will the mom give up and no longer care? In some children's lives, the bond that once existed will one day be ripped away. Cries of pain in the bed at night will go unheard. Things will have drastically changed.

Whereas Mom used to search for her missing child, now she no longer calls or searches when the child is not at home. The child eats at home alone. He or she crosses the threshold of a cold and unaccompanied dwelling alone and afraid. "Where did Mom go?" the child asks. "Where are you, Momma?" he or she cries.

In search for the feeling of existence, satisfaction, and survival, the child replaces the safe haven of the home for a new playground called the streets. The child has his or her own breath, and the voices that he or she hears are many. He or she understands now that in this life, he or she is on his or her own; without a mother, the child's world is spinning into confusion because he or she is but a youth. The love once shared with the mother has been ripped away and has seemingly ended. For one reason or another, the mother fails to recognize that her child desperately needs her. The child is excited to see anyone, any someone who will care. The child is growing empty inside and wants to feel loved, be hugged, and once again sit in his or her own mother's lap. Though the child needs her, she is not there. The child wonders, "Who am I?" The sad response: a latchkey child.

Many children have experienced a painful death without a weapon. When a mother's love is missing in a young child's life, it kills the child deep from within. Probably the number one human need is to be and to feel loved. The lack of a mother's love is one way to give the streets an opportunity to step in and take over this young child's thinking. Dysfunction will continue to breed dysfunction.

Have you ever seen a child unloved by his or her mother? There are many pent-up emotions in the mind of this individual. Manifestations of these emotions appear in many different ways. What is it like for this child to feel hated or abandoned by the one who is supposed to love him or her? How does he or she handle being discriminated against in his or her own home? Love is not always expressed properly with words, but a child cannot mistake what he or she sees and feels. What happened, what made this one child the black sheep of the family? Why is this child treated differently from all of the other siblings when they all came from the same womb? In some families, there is the unwanted and emotionally abused child, the ugly duckling. Sometimes parents put all of their eggs into one basket so to speak by treating one child significantly better or apparently different from the others. This attitude promotes tremendous rivalries between siblings. Anger grows inside and becomes dangerous because it has no outlet. The unloved, unwanted, unplanned child becomes vulnerable to the forces and voices of evil. Why was this child simply not good enough? Why was this child different? Have you ever read the story about "The Child Called IT"? A Book written by Dave Pelzer. "Dave Pelzer was brutally beaten and starved by his emotionally unstable, alcoholic mother, a mother who played tortuous, unpredictable games ¿ games that left one of her three sons nearly dead. She no longer considered Dave a son, but a slave; no longer a boy, but an ¿it¿.His bed was an old army cot in the basement, his clothes were torn and smelly, and when he was allowed the luxury of food it was scraps from the dog¿s bowl. The outside world knew nothing of the nightmare played out behind closed doors. But throughout Dave kept alive dreams of finding a family to love him. This book covers the early years of his life and is an affecting an inspirational book of the horrors of child abuse and the steadfast determination of one child to survive."[8]

Hatred produces hatred, vengeance, and intolerance. Let us talk for a moment about the children who found love on the streets and now have matured into young adults. They have found what they once searched for: the very emotion that was lacking inside of their homes, love. They find it on the streets and in gangs, who drag them into situations that will possibly be the end of their lives or send them to jail. Love is just that strong, and they are willing to take the risk just to find it. For these children, the people that love them the most are involved in violent crimes, theft, and murder. These violent offenders on the streets perhaps also sought love at one time and found it lacking in their homes. Sadly, there seems to be a vicious cycle of dysfunction.

Perhaps this love is missing because some of these mothers were unloved themselves. Conceivably, they do not know how to love. What a sad commentary on life. I believe that the dark-skinned African American woman is the least respected and most unloved human being on the face of this earth. She has been through so many struggles, and they continue with no end in sight. She is perhaps the most unloved

8   http://books.google.com/books/about/A_Child_Called_It.html?id=zFLWQwAACAAJ
     Edition 2, reprint
     Publisher Orion Publishing Group, 2001
     ISBN 0752837508, 9780752837505
     2012 Google
     Title A Child Called 'It'
     Author Dave J. Pelzer

of all of the children in our society because of the darker shade of her skin. There are so many different shades of brown skin found within the African American race. Perhaps this is the reason that discrimination and prejudice against African Americans also exist by African Americans.

The best way for mothers to keep their children off the streets is to love them with all of their hearts and to never allow the streets' demonstration of love to ever be exemplified as stronger than hers. She should be involved in her child's life every step of the way. It worked best when mothers were at home when their children arrived from school and they shared in family times and family days. In my opinion, a mother should be interested in her children's likes, dislikes, hobbies, and crafts. The instruction, wisdom, and love of a mother should give the child purpose, direction, and most of all, God. Eating together as a family and keeping the lines of communication open bring great rewards. Mothers should discipline their children diligently and consistently. Without these and other similar things like these in place, children feel unloved, and an unloved child causes the death of that child without a weapon. The lack of love slowly kills them from within.

CHAPTER 6

RESPECT

Why is respect so necessary and needed in urban communities? Better yet, why does humanity demand so much of it? Whatever the answer is, its need is so strong that some will do just about anything to gain it. Jackie Robinson once said, "I'm not concerned with your liking or disliking me ... All I ask is that you respect me as a human being." The feeling of being disrespected is like being spit in the face.

Many violent crimes committed among adolescents in the inner cities are to gain a level of respect from their peers. Without the respect of his or her peers, the social order and status that an individual hoped for becomes an impossible goal. Respect is worth its weight in gold. It is more necessary and beneficial than the mighty dollar. As people travel through urban areas, it is respect that allows them the freedom to roam. Wannabes make the inner cities the most dangerous and difficult places to live because they desire a name for themselves. They seek out the most violent crimes to commit, which will boost their image and puff them up. Respect is closely associated to arrogance and pride. Most inner-city tenants know that arrogance and pride are very destructive in so many ways and on so many different levels.

Respect is coupled together with value and self-worth. Respect or the lack of it stimulates the emotions in both negative and positive thinking. Respect is pursued because of pride. An individual wants to be heard and desires to be counted. An individual wants to end the day with his or her dignity intact. A person's dignity is nearly worth everything and extremely valuable to most men and women.

African Americans, like all people, need to feel and to be respected. African American men and women have been treated so inhumanly for so long that it has had a crippling effect. Imagine being stripped of all pride and dignity. Imagine being treated as a lower-class citizen and being continually ridiculed. Imagine being treated with less respect than an animal; a dog could drink from a water fountain, but a black person could not. A dog could enter through the front door, but the African Americans had to enter through the rear. African American lives were meaningless and of very little value. African Americans could be killed, but they could not retaliate in self-defense. The draft forced an African American to go to war to defend a country that had a tremendous hatred and disdain for him. Some refused induction into the service because the enemy, which is racial prejudice, of the African American manifested itself in America. This brings the reader to the famous words of Muhammad Ali, "Ain't no Vietcong ever called me nigger." Think Exist.com a website filled with quotes records, Even Malcolm X had issues with the idea of going to war against a foreign enemy. It only makes sense to desire justice at home. As Malcolm X stated in defense of the African American who had been beaten, battered, killed, and bruised, "If violence is wrong in America, violence is wrong abroad. If it is wrong to be violent defending black women and black children and black babies and black men, then it is wrong for America to draft us, and make us violent abroad in defense of her. And if it is right for America to draft us and teach us how to be violent in defense of her, then it is right for you and me to do whatever is necessary to defend our own people right here in this country."

The moral standards of America seem to have been fixed so that Caucasians in America always have the advantage. The black man was aggressively stripped of all of his rights, pride, and dignity. And some wonder why so many African Americans are angry almost to the point of rage at the injustice that continues. Many blacks lack the desire to trust in a society that has for so many years been against them.

The Tuskegee syphilis experiment (also known as the Tuskegee syphilis study or Public Health Service syphilis study) and the Port Chicago incident are two examples of how inhumanely African Americans have been treated in this country. As reported by Wikipedia:

> The Tuskegee syphilis experiment[1] was an infamous
> clinical study conducted between 1932 and 1972 by

the U.S. Public Health Service to study the natural progression of untreated syphilis in rural African American men who thought they were receiving free health care from the U.S. government.[1]

The Public Health Service, working with the Tuskegee Institute, began the study in 1932. Investigators enrolled in the study a total of 600 impoverished sharecroppers from Macon County, Alabama; 399 who had previously contracted syphilis before the study began, and 201[2] without the disease. For participating in the study, the men were given free medical care, meals, and free burial insurance. They were never told they had syphilis, nor were they ever treated for it. According to the Centers for Disease Control, the men were told they were being treated for "bad blood", a local term for various illnesses that include syphilis, anemia, and fatigue.

The 40-year study was controversial for reasons related to ethical standards; primarily because researchers knowingly failed to treat patients appropriately after the 1940s validation of penicillin as an effective cure for the disease they were studying. Revelation of study failures by a whistleblower led to major changes in U.S. law and regulation on the protection of participants in clinical studies....[9]

The website of the Centers for Disease Control and Prevention provides the following information about the study:

In 1932, the Public Health Service, working with the Tuskegee Institute, began a study to record the natural history of syphilis in hopes of justifying treatment programs for blacks. It was called the "Tuskegee Study of Untreated Syphilis in the Negro Male....

In July 1972, an Associated Press story about the Tuskegee Study caused a public outcry that led the

---

9   From Wikipedia, the free encyclopedia, http://en.wikipedia.org/wiki/Tuskegee syphilis experiment#cite note-timeline-0. Wikipedia® is a registered trademark of the Wikipedia Foundation, Inc., a nonprofit organization.

Assistant Secretary for Health and Scientific Affairs to appoint an Ad Hoc Advisory Panel to review the study. The panel had nine members from the fields of medicine, law, religion, labor, education, health administration, and public affairs.

The panel found that the men had agreed freely to be examined and treated. However, there was no evidence that researchers had informed them of the study or its real purpose. In fact, the men had been misled and had not been given all the facts required to provide informed consent.

The men were never given adequate treatment for their disease. Even when penicillin became the drug of choice for syphilis in 1947, researchers did not offer it to the subjects. The advisory panel found nothing to show that subjects were ever given the choice of quitting the study, even when this new, highly effective treatment became widely used.[10]

My grandfather was one of the many African American men who died under this study. My father and his three siblings were not involved in the study but were given a total of approximately $1,000.00 from the government as a death benefit to share. The amount of this death benefit demonstrates the value placed upon and the respect given to African Americans.

I have added the Port Chicago incident because, though the government blames these navy men for being incompetent, many additional theories have come to the surface. The major suspicion and conspiracy allegation is that the Port Chicago incident was no accident at all.

The *Port Chicago Naval Magazine* describes the background of this incident as follows:

Construction at Port Chicago began in 1942. By 1944, expansion and improvements to the pier could support the loading of two ships simultaneously.

---

10   The Tuskegee Timeline, http://www.cdc.gov/tuskegee/timeline.htm. Centers for Disease Control and Prevention, 1600 Clifton Rd., Atlanta, GA 30333, cdcinfo@cdc.gov.

African-American Navy personnel units were assigned to the dangerous work at Port Chicago. Reflecting the racial segregation of the day, the officers of these units were white. The officers and men had received some training in cargo handling, but not in loading munitions. The bulk of their experience came from hands-on experience. Loading went on around the clock. The Navy ordered that proper regulations for working with munitions be followed.[11]

The US Navy issued an order regarding proper regulations to men who had not been trained. As a result, 4,606 tons of explosives detonated, killing many and wounding others. The explosion was felt from San Francisco to Nevada. The 7,200-ton ship was destroyed, and it like many other close objects became unrecognizable. Many believe that the incident was completely avoidable.

Aretha Franklin wrote in her song "All I'm asking is for a little respect when I come home." During slavery, racial segregation, and even the unfair treatment of today, respect is something that African Americans have been determined to gain. During the days of slavery, the slave owner raped black women without an earthly penalty. There were no laws of protection for the African American. These men and women were disrespected, devalued, degraded, and dishonored. African American families were split and divided. Both children and adults were sold, separating them from loved ones. What kind of person would do such a thing? It has been taught that blacks have evolved from apes and cannot learn because they have smaller brains. In addition, there was the teaching that the African American had no soul.

Some universities and colleges are still teaching a false dogma regarding human beings. The very idea that a human has evolved is an absolute farce to our human thinking. Yet people who are considered intelligent have been caught in the middle of a tremendous controversy that has no factual or scientific evidence. The controversy over the

11 Port Chicago Naval Magazine Explosion, 1944, Department of the Navy—Naval Historical Center, 805 Kidder Breese SE, Washington Navy Yard, Washington, DC 20374-5060. Adapted from: National Park Service, *Port Chicago Naval Magazine*, Washington: Government Printing Office, n.d. [a set of two brochures]. 1 June 2005. http://www.history.navy.mil/faqs/faq80-1.htm.

origin of the species has continued even until this day and will probably exist until racism is abolished from the hearts and minds of humanity.

Charles Darwin, author of the book *The Descent of Man*, made decisions about humanity that to this day have not been proven and in fact are nothing more than a theory. He was convinced that the Caucasian race was and is superior to all others. He believed that African Americans and Australians had not fully developed, making them inferior. To make his theory even more degrading and sexist, he believed that all women were inferior to men. Even animals were considered by him and his followers to be of a much greater value than the "negro."

How does a human being transition from such hatred, anger, violent aggression, and deceit? Where is the hope? Perhaps if hope were restored or if blacks trusted and believed that there actually were a way to be educated at an affordable cost and receive good jobs with equal pay, gang violence would decline and crime would decrease among African Americans. Why would crime decrease and gangs dwindle away? Hope is the answer. Hope in the mind of a human being that has been reestablished and sown into the heart does amazing things. Hope is not painting the streets of the inner cities. Paint on buildings and streets only gives the neighborhood an external cleansing, never an internal one. If these inner-city residents could witness real change in their communities or move to a different environment, seeing life from a different perspective, hope might possibly be restored. Perhaps if African Americans could feel and see a nation as a whole that truly cared for all her citizens alike, hope might begin to be restored.

When a person visualizes something he or she has never seen before, it intrigues the mind. Consider the effects of the beauty of nature on the human mind when seen for the first time by an inner-city child. A ride into the country, for example, or a ride on streets where chaos is limited—that, my friend, is a true blessing. It opens one's eyes to an entirely different world. Nature seems to affect the mind in an amazingly positive way. Nature shows the world in another light. It shows equality, justice, and a lack of partiality. It is amazing that a brown chicken can hatch a white egg. Look at the compassion of a mother lioness with her cubs. Observe and witness the tenderness of a female crocodile as she places her young into her jaws of death. We witness true unity and great teamwork observing a pack of wild dogs as they hunt. Closely examine the loveliness of a butterfly, which gracefully flies through the sky. The heavens display her beauty as the clouds expand and decorate the skies.

The stars show light in the midst of darkness. The four seasons bring positive change. The summer's sun brings heat to enjoy and the gift of the day. Many enjoy the oceans, lakes, creeks, and refreshing streams of water. Fall brings a beautiful array of absolutely mesmerizing colors. The winter's cold brings relatives indoors to enjoy the closeness of family. The spring causes people to leap for joy as new life begins. How many inner-city children have ever gone on this blissful journey? Every inner-city child would benefit from this great opportunity to experience nature at its best. A change needs to come; a change is going to come.

Perhaps the media has done African Americans a great injustice. Blacks are displayed as violent aggressors and a people to be feared. The suggestion is that African Americans cannot be trusted. Subliminally, it has been displayed through the media that African Americans are the dregs of society. The image that is drawn is that blacks are not good enough or are inferior. In public schools, black history is taught for one month out of the year. True history should include all races and be taught throughout the entire year. Ignorance is an amazing animal. The less that society knows about the good that African Americans have done, the more control an adversary has over them. In comparison, how often are blacks put on display in a positive light for doing good deeds? Is it rare because blacks rarely do good deeds, or is it intentionally and maliciously overlooked?

As a result, when blacks visit public establishments, they seem to be put on display. Security, security cameras, clerks, and even simple employees are told to watch out for, well, you know, a thief. Who has the media profiled as the thief? Apparently, the thief is the shopper with a darker skin. Coincidentally, even today, the African American man is diligently followed through the stores and watched very carefully.

The African American is dishonored even in the world of animation. Who are the superheroes and great ones of the earth? One might call African Americans the villains instead of the heroes. The saviors of the world in fictional movies, comic strips, and cartoons seem to be Caucasians. Why is that? There are only a few black superheroes—like the Green Lantern, Black Panther, Storm, Black Goliath, Falcon, Steel, Bishop, Captain Marvel, Night Thrasher War Machine, Luke Cage, Frozone, Black Lightning, and Power Man. Most of these mentioned were not portrayed as real heroes or superheroes. There are hundreds and maybe thousands of "real" superheroes, but only a few are black. Blacks have attempted to come up with present-day superheroes, but to no avail. Even the pictures of Jesus and strong good Bible characters are painted as white. Jesus was a Jew.

Did African Americans have a part in any of America's wars helping her to gain the victory? Yes, they had a tremendous impact helping to bring freedom and independence to America. Where are the movies and pictures of these heroes? What heroic actions and great sacrifices did they make for the country? The widely spread message is that African Americans have not contributed much to this land of the free.

Why are there African Americans and not just Americans? Caucasians are not called White Americans or Caucasian Americans. Why not? Both African Americans and Caucasian Americans originate from foreign lands. America was inhabited before Columbus arrived. Caucasians too are immigrants. Society has a double standard. What is good for one is not good for another.

As a result of Darwin's dogmatic teachings, racial inequality, and segregation, nonwhites were treated inhumanely. Blacks in particular became the targets for lynchings and attacks by government agencies. Our fathers were sprayed with high-pressure hoses and attacked by police dogs. African Americans attempted many nonviolent ways to end this unnecessary brutality. Marches, protests, and rallies were organized and brought a measure of change. Finally, the voices of those in the struggle were heard, but not without tremendous resistance and hardened hearts. Some voices, like Thurgood Marshall's, were heard through the courts; Dr. Martin Luther King through the churches; Roy Wilkins, director of the NAACP, through the media; and Malcolm X in the public's eyes and through the streets. The number of workers both at the forefront and behind the scenes are too numerous to count. Know this one thing: African Americans were fed up and demanding change. Their voices were heard by government and in the courts. In 1948, President Harry Truman introduced fair employment laws in the government, including the military, for all US citizens.

Although these laws were in effect, the hatred of African Americans did not cease. The hearts of some white Americans did not change. "James H. Meredith, who in 1962 became the first African American to attend the University of Mississippi, is shot by a sniper shortly after beginning a lone civil rights march through the South. Known as the

"March Against Fear," Meredith had been walking from Memphis, Tennessee, to Jackson, Mississippi, in an attempt to encourage voter registration by African Americans in the South."[12] There were many grotesque executions because of the color of a person's skin. Yes, this was a dark time in America's history. Black men and women were torn down and continually humiliated. Where could one go for protection, equality, or liberty?

To make matters worse, many laws superseded judicial law, these being given the term "Jim Crow laws." The "Jim Crow Laws" in my opinion were written because of the fear of African American men. They were designed to protect the Caucasian's and to shield them from any negative economic, religious or civil down turn. "Jim Crow laws empowered racist groups and gave them authority to violate all legislative laws without the fear of retaliation from the government or minorities. No African American was exempt, even children were governed by these laws. Though the examples of injustice are too numerous to count, the reader is reminded of the shameful case in Money, Mississippi, 1955 with the young 14 year old Emmett Louis Till who was beaten beyond description for his violation of a "Jim Crow Law" regarding white women. Are these times what some Americans call today, "The Good Old Days?"

Dr. David Pilgrim, Professor of Sociology describes the "Jim Crow Laws" as follows.

"The following Jim Crow etiquette norms show how inclusive and pervasive these norms were: A black male could not offer his hand (to shake hands) with a white male because it implied being socially equal. Obviously, a black male could not offer his hand or any other part of his body to a white woman, because he risked being accused of rape. Blacks and whites were not supposed to eat together. If they did eat together, whites were to be served first, and some sort of partition was to

12   http://www.history.com/this-day-in-history/james-meredith-shot
     History.com
     This Day In History
     Jun 6, 1966:
     James Meredith shot
     © 1996-2013, A&E Television Networks, LLC. All Rights Reserved.Jofreeman.com,

be placed between them. Under no circumstance was a black male to offer to light the cigarette of a white female -- that gesture implied intimacy. Blacks were not allowed to show public affection toward one another in public, especially kissing, because it offended whites. Jim Crow etiquette prescribed that blacks were introduced to whites, never whites to blacks. For example: "Mr. Peters (the white person), this is Charlie (the black person), that I spoke to you about." Whites did not use courtesy titles of respect when referring to blacks, for example, Mr., Mrs., Miss., Sir, or Ma'am. Instead, blacks were called by their first names. Blacks had to use courtesy titles when referring to whites, and were not allowed to call them by their first names. If a black person rode in a car driven by a white person, the black person sat in the back seat, or the back of a truck. White motorists had the right-of-way at all intersections. Stetson Kennedy, the author of Jim Crow Guide (1990), offered these simple rules that blacks were supposed to observe in conversing with whites: 1.Never assert or even intimate that a white person is lying. 2. Never impute dishonorable intentions to a white person. 3. Never suggest that a white person is from an inferior class. 4. Never lay claim to, or overly demonstrate, superior knowledge or intelligence. 5. Never curse a white person. 6. Never laugh derisively at a white person. 7. Never comment upon the appearance of a white female."[13.]

What country is opening the doors and saying to the African American, "Come, you are welcome here?" What country can an African American flee to? Where can the African American go and

---

13 Jim Crow Museum of Racist Memorabilia
"Using Objects Of Intolerance to teach Tolerance and Promote Social Justice"
© Dr. David Pilgrim, Professor of Sociology
Ferris State University
Sept., 2000
Edited 2012
http://www.ferris.edu/jimcrow/what.htm

be left alone, without ridicule or prejudice, and feel at peace? I would venture to say that the only safe haven for all people is heaven. The media aids in the world's hatred toward African Americans, showing black faces and the darker skin mostly in the negative and rarely in the positive. Blacks are rarely the heroes who save a city or nation, but mostly the villains. Neither African Americans nor just plain Africans are consistently portrayed as the good neighbor next door; they are often portrayed as the one who destroys a neighborhood. Blacks are portrayed as gangbangers, drug dealers, ignorant, descendants of animals, violent aggressors, thieves, without souls, poor—the dregs of society. What is the African to do? With a false slanderous reputation like this, where and how can the African find respect?

Some in the world today do not like the African, and so maybe that is why some African Americans dislike African Americans! Blacks have become enemies of blacks. Yes, African Americans have demonstrated hatred toward their own race. This idea will be illustrated in the next chapter.

CHAPTER 7

BLACK-ON-BLACK CRIMES

Is it possible for a people to become so despondent that killing one another becomes sport? The African American man of yesteryear had to dig deep just to earn a little respect. Just the respect of calling him by his name instead of being referred to as "boy" was considered an achievement. Times were tough, but these African American men and women were, as one would say, as tough as nails, strong and durable. They respected each other and learned how to cooperate and work together. This cooperation lasted all of the way through the civil rights movement. There were many different organized movements striving to end segregation, like boycotts, sit-ins, marches, strikes, and the legal system through the courts, just to name a few. Though these movements approached a solution in different ways, they all had one common goal: equality. Blacks simply wanted equity. Justice was demanded, though injustice and fraud were the way of the day toward African Americans. Though true equality has not yet been achieved, our ancestors did a marvelous work with the help of God to get us to where we are today. The torch has been passed on, but who is willing to carry it?

What problems do we face today? Evil seeds of superiority and inferiority have been implanted into the human mind. While some Caucasians try to hold onto superiority in their own minds, some minorities are struggling with inferiority in theirs. How can the perceived inferior become equal to the perceived superior?

"In the "doll test," psychologists Kenneth and Mamie Clark used four plastic, diaper-clad dolls, identical except for color. They showed the dolls to black children between the ages of three and seven and asked them questions to determine racial perception and preference. Almost all of the children readily identified the race of the dolls. However, when asked which they preferred, the majority selected the white doll and attributed positive characteristics to it. The Clarks also gave the children outline drawings of a boy and girl and asked them to color the figures the same color as themselves. Many of the children with dark complexions colored the figures with a white or yellow crayon. The Clarks concluded that "prejudice, discrimination, and segregation" caused black children to develop a sense of inferiority and self-hatred."[14]

The Clarks were right. "Prejudice, discrimination, and segregation" breed a tremendous amount of "inferiority and self-hatred." In the experiment, the white dolls were affirmed as both pretty and nice, while the black doll was declared bad and ugly. It has been my opinion for years as I have examined and studied the general behavior of the African American race, in some cases, we seem to dislike each other and perhaps even ourselves. African Americans have usually been kind and partial to other races but cruel and contemptible to their own. It seems as though when some African Americans get their foot past the door and are surrounded by Caucasian colleagues, they forget where they have come from and who they are. They forget that they are still African Americans.

In 2003, CNN's Anderson Cooper repeated the test. "A white child looks at a picture of a black child and says she's bad because she's black. A black child says a white child is ugly because he's white. A white child says a black child is dumb because she has dark skin."[15] In other words the self-taught problem of race relations has not gone away.

This seed of hatred for self has grown so deep inside of the hearts of African Americans that killing each other seems not to be a problem at all. African Americans are exterminating their own race because of such hostility, anger, and hopelessness. In spite of the past, we have to change!

---

14 Brown *v.* Board of Education, The Library of Congress, 101 Independence Ave., S.E., Washington D.C. 20540-1400.
http://www.loc.gov/exhibits/brown/brown-brown.html

15 *Madison Gray Time Magazine,* in partnership with CNN. Anderson Cooper Study: White and black children biased toward lighter skin
May 14, 2010 4:24 p.m. EDT
http://www.cnn.com/2010/US/05/13/doll.study/index.html

There seems to be a civil war going on inside of America, one civilization or community against another. The hatred and killing are both ruthless and senseless. Black-on-black crime has reached an epidemic level. It has reached the rich and the poor, the famous and infamous. This hatred exists in the ghetto and suburbs and on the hills. After leaving the US Army, I enrolled in college. During those days, I continued my military service in the US Army National Guard and served during the Rodney King riots. I lived in South Central, Los Angeles, on La Salle Avenue with two of my many mentors and brethren, Fred and Welton Hickman. The riots began a few blocks from their home. I was in Buena Park; school was in session at the time the verdict was announced. Both faculty and students pleaded with me not to go home, but I refused. The trial was not in South Central; it was in Simi Valley.

First, let me say that I am not a supporter of violence in any way, but hope to use this event to help prove my point. Because of self-hatred, African Americans will do to themselves things that they will not do to others. Instead of going to Simi Valley and destroying the neighborhood where the trial and residents lived, the black community destroyed itself. Our houses were filled with smoke as buildings were burned to the ground. Our community was affected in every way. What point did the residents of Los Angeles actually get across to America? While I agree an injustice was done, the riots poured salt onto an open wound. They hurt their own people and demolished their own community. Jobs were lost and banking ceased. Stores were looted and burned to the ground. There were no police officers in our communities for three days. The fire departments, which were attempting to tend to the local fires, were unable to do their jobs because of rapid gunfire; the fire departments were the targets. African Americans were in rage, but at whom? Whom could be blamed for these actions?

I am not in any way attempting to justify the actions of law enforcement, and likewise I am not justifying the actions of the blacks involved in the riots. It is a fact that police brutality, racial profiling, and excessive force have been an ongoing problem in the United States, and the acquittal of these officers was absolutely abhorrent. How could the courts justify officers mercilessly beating a man pulled over for a speeding violation? The end result of the actions of these corrupt officers was multiple deaths, looting, fire, destruction, and crime. When those who are responsible to uphold the law, break the law, devastation follows. However, the question is whom can the African American blame for burning down their own communities? The public structures were not to blame, and the senseless beating of Reginald Denny cannot be justified. Those involved can blame no one but themselves. All races of people hurt themselves when they do not respect themselves. They beat up, murder, rape, and destroy themselves because they hate who they are. Friends, brothers, and fellow human beings, are there no other ways to exist as a people?

Michael Jackson wrote a very controversial song entitled "They Don't Care About Us," bringing criticism mostly in America regarding its lyrics. These lyrics demonstrate the fact that racism and racial inequality still exist on every level. Mr. Jackson speaks of being beaten, hated, and enslaved. I have selected a few lines from his lyrics to illustrate my point. "Beat me, hate me. You can never break me... I am the victim of police brutality, now I'm tired of bein the victim of hate ... black man, black male, throw your brother in jail ... All I wanna say is that, they don't really care about us ..."[16]

---

16 Michael Jackson song "They Don't Really Care About Us; album *HIStory: Past, Present and Future, Book I*, released on April 1, 1996.

CHAPTER 8

THE CRAB THEORY

The crab theory originates with the actions and activity of crabs, the crabs that have ten legs and claws. I remember crabs from the East Coast. In Maryland, we enjoyed blue crabs at a restaurant called the "Chesapeake Bay." We ate crab cakes with delight. A brief study of crabs will help the reader to understand how this principle relates to human beings.

Pinching, pulling, and snapping crabs never require a lid on a bucket. Crabs cannot escape from a bucket simply because they do not possess the skill of teamwork. Instead of linking together and ultimately pulling each other to the top, they seem to instinctually pull each other down. They grab the legs of another crab that has a legitimate chance of reaching the top of the bucket and pull that crab down literally to the bottom of the pile.

Another of those concepts that inner-city children have heard and been taught repeatedly is a word that no one from the urban community wants placed on himself or herself; the word is *sellout*. No one wants to be a sellout. A sellout is someone who makes it out of his community alive and well, gets a higher education or some corporate job, and no longer hangs out with his boys as he did in his past. Sellouts disassociate themselves from their past path of life, friends, and community. The so-called sellouts no longer hang because they have made money and appear to act and to portray themselves as better than others. However, those in their community knew them before they were what they are today. The term sellout will hold its captives in the ghetto *forever*!

In Jay Z's song entitled "New York," he declared himself "hood forever," which means that though he has made it big, he remains the same.

What is wrong with people growing up, being more mature, no longer thuggin' or hanging out on the streets, banging and taunting the police as many once did? The so-called idea of selling out in my opinion is only wrong if a person is bound to the idea that any form of success defines the individual as selling out. All eyes are on the inner-city man or woman when he or she makes that change or transformation. Others want to know what he or she will do with this new life. Old acquaintances want that inner-city friendship and relationship forever. There is nothing wrong with desiring a lasting relationship. However, the rules and boundaries of that relationship must change with time and maturity. The building blocks of a relationship in the urban community are deep because of the many traumatic experiences that inner-city youths have gone through together. Relationships run deep because of incarceration, violence, and the loss of so many lives during their lifetimes. The strong bond of family has been developed, and the family that was at one time resilient has grown weak because of the death and incarceration of its membership at a young age. The bond is not a bond of gangs, but the powerful bond of unity.

I joined the military because I thought that this choice was my only way out. My boys thought that I was crazy and couldn't understand why I wanted to leave. Four days before I was scheduled to leave for boot camp in the US Army, my life was to take a drastic turn. "Celebrity Hall," also known as "The Black Hole," in Northwest DC could have been the last place that I was seen alive. I refused to leave Eric's side, though, and he refused to leave mine. It was a night that our bond became even stronger and one that we would never forget. The good Lord was watching out for us then as He is to this day. Obviously, the events that followed did not end in our deaths, and we live to tell the story if we so choose. Perhaps one day in the future this story and many other experiences will be shared by friends and relatives.

The idea of a sellout is a thought that holds one down. While attempting to be true to one's culture and old life at the same time, one still strives to get ahead. There is this huge weight or burden limiting one's ability to move ahead. In order to remove oneself from the cyclic pattern of destruction, the chain of bondage must be broken. The break must be clean. By instinct, crabs never allow other crabs out of the bucket, but human beings do it by choice.

Young adults have to learn how to move ahead without reaching back into their past. How is that possible without forgetting their loved ones and those who existed in very important times of their lives? I think that the answer is very clear: never forget and take along all who are willing to follow. Sadly, those who have no desire to change must be left behind. Here is where the decision to break the chain can be made without regret, but it takes strength and inward resolve.

If a young adult shares his or her dreams and aspirations, others may be inclined to follow. The friends and associates who disbelieve that dream will not fault him or her for dreaming big dreams. Dreamers and idealists must be careful not to allow others to destroy those dreams through persecution and ridicule. By sharing one's dreams and aspirations, one is not selling out but moving ahead. One is not moving ahead without sharing the knowledge that he or she has discovered. Instead of being called a sellout, he is named "College Boy" or given a respectful name representing positive change. The hard part is not being drawn back into that past lifestyle. Those who do not share in his or her dreams and remain behind will have no problem welcoming him or her back the day he or she grows weak and wants to return. In fact, they will test him or her to determine his or her sincerity and the level of his or her commitment. By the grace of God, I have made it out of that lifestyle, and I have no intention of returning; all whom I knew and know are welcome to follow me if they so desire. However, I must admit that there was a time that I was almost drawn back in. I thank God for saving me and using my friend and "boy" Eric Lee to keep me away. Oh, and by the way, he too is doing very well for himself.

In closing this chapter, I would like to introduce you to a man whose life demonstrates a true transition, change, and reform. His name is Stanley Williams.

Stanley "Tookie" Williams is a great example and picture of leaving the past life, moving forward, and attempting to take as many who are willing along with him. He was strong and determined to make a difference. He turned his negative strength into the positive. Stanley Williams probably started out as most inner-city children, hanging out with his boys and eventually culminating into the Los Angeles gang known as the Crips.

On Tuesday, 13 December the co-founder of one of the world's biggest gangs, a man convicted of murdering

41

four people, will be led into a small room in the depths of San Quentin prison in San Francisco Bay.

The bodybuilder who terrorized 1970s South Central Los Angeles with his "Crips" gang will be strapped to a medical table, and a lethal injection will bring Stanley "Tookie" Williams' 24 years on death row to an end. He knows he has done wrong in his life, but he still proclaims his innocence. Behind him he will leave five Nobel peace prize nominations, a letter from President George W Bush commending him on his work, and a movie portraying his life called, simply, Redemption.[17]

After realizing his mistakes, Williams felt obligated to reach out to young people, with a message debunking the glorified image of gang membership. He decided to channel his message through a series of children's books entitled *Tookie Speaks Out*. In 1996 Barbara Becnel, Williams's co-author, sold the idea for the children's books to the Rosen Publishing Group and the wheels were in motion to distribute Williams's books, which he wrote and then dictated to Becnel.

The books were used in schools and juvenile correction facilities in the United States, Africa, and Switzerland, and have drawn attention from people across the country. All the proceeds from Williams's books have gone to non-profit organizations including Mothers Against Gang Violence, a group based in South Central. Dr. Allen Cohen, executive director of Pacific Institute for Research and Evaluation, was prompted to contact Williams and Becnel about launching other anti-gang measures in schools after reading the "Tookie" books. "The themes in the book were entirely congruent with what I think is the best knowledge of

---

17   "Reformed Gang Leader Awaits Death," by Alistair Leithead,
      BBC News, Last Updated: Thursday, 1 December 2005, 17:27 GMT,
      http://news.bbc.co.uk/2/hi/americas/4486178.stm
      http://www.bbc.co.uk/aboutthebbc/BBC.

the potential of young people to get associated with negative behavior," Cohen said in *Los Angeles Times*.[18]

Tookie was executed by lethal injection on December 13, 2005. In my opinion, America should have allowed him clemency because of the number of lives he had changed, which speaks to the number of crimes and senseless murders that he prevented. Who knows the good that he could have done from behind the prison bars of San Quentin? Society must destroy the statement, "You can take the boy out of the hood but you cannot take the hood out of the boy."

---

18   Who2 Profiles. Copyright © 1998–2011 by Who2, LLC. All rights reserved.
Stanley Tookie Williams biography.
Shellie M. Saunders and Jennifer M. York
Copyright © 2011 Answers Corporation,
http://www.answers.com/topic/stanley-williams#ixzz1GRQd22Dl.

CHAPTER 9
THE ILLUSION FACTOR

Normally when humans think of illusions, they think of the secret art of magic. Most people love a good magic trick. They love to be fooled and misled by card tricks and things disappearing right before their eyes. Adults know that magic is sleight of hand, but that does not change the desire to see and to be fooled for just a moment.

Being misled by the art of magic is one thing, but could we also be comfortable with societal illusions as well? The lottery, for example, carries with it a heavy illusion. People know that someone will be the winner of hundreds, thousands, and at times millions of dollars, but only one can win. Citizens are drawn in with the hopes and dreams of being that one winner, knowing that the odds are against them.

Though race relations are somewhat better than years gone by throughout the world, we must admit that a problem still exists. The behavior of some Americans has given the illusion that there is no longer a problem and that our dysfunction as a nation has been solved. Though some try to hide it, the entire world knows different. South African Archbishop Desmond Tutu said, "'In your country, race … is a very, very real issue. And I think on the whole you keep trying to pretend it isn't,' he added, noting the issue will haunt Americans until there is a way to talk honestly about race, such as holding a reconciliation forum."[19]

---

19 "Desmond Tutu: Equality of U.S. Blacks an 'Illusion,'" May 14, 2008, by Storer H. Rowley, *Chicago Tribune*, Chicagotribune.com, 435 Michigan Avenue, Chicago, IL 60611. http://articles.chicagotribune.com/2008-05-14/news/0805130608_1_truth-and-reconciliation-commission-african-american-real-issue.

America still has a major problem and a long way to go in solving this dilemma. The first solution is to be open and honest, and the second is to care enough to get involved. Perhaps society is her own worst enemy. There is so much to give, learn, and gain from each other, but the desire to cross color and race lines rarely exists. The world has many conveniences because of new inventions and modern technology. Inventors of the world are from all races and colors, with many things to share. Yet some Americans refuse to give in. As Rodney King once said, "Can't we all just get along?"

The danger of illusions is how people look at themselves. Perception is an amazing concept. One might continually ask the question, "What does the world expect of me?" If we take any race or group of people, define them, and through the media give society's expectations of them, that is most likely what they will become, prove, or aspire to be. If people mistreat others and teach others that they are animals, they will likely act according to the expectations. There are stigmas placed on just about every group of people because humans love to judge. Someone once said, "Walk a mile in my shoes," and maybe that is it: people need to walk in others' shoes before they judge or persecute them.

Here is additional information on Mr. Tookie.

> Williams was raised by his mother—his father left when Williams was a toddler. Without a father figure, he learned about black men through stereotypes that labeled them as violent, promiscuous, and criminal. Williams internalized those negative stereotypes and grew up, as he told the *San Francisco Chronicle*, "mimicking pimps and drug dealers." As a teenager, he rarely attended high school. By the age of 16, he had already earned a reputation outside of the classroom as a street warrior on the South Central's west side. Williams told *Contemporary Black Biography* he was considered a "bully slayer" because he fought kids who picked on his relatives and friends.[20]

20 Who2 Profiles. Copyright © 1998–2011 by Who2, LLC.
See the Stanley Tookie Williams biography from Who2.
Shellie M. Saunders and Jennifer M. York
http://www.answers.com/topic/stanley-williams#ixzz1GRQd22Dl.
Copyright © 2011 Answers Corporation

"A couple of factors that work against young black men is their portrayal in the media as gangsters, thugs and rappers on the fringes of society, and the fact that more black men are going to prison than college, according to a report by the U.S. Justice Department."[21]

In America, there is the illusion of equal opportunities. Yet when African Americans go to the bank for loans and look for opportunities to get ahead, there is a definite awakening. Trying to buy a home is tough, and most young African Americans do not believe that they will ever become eligible. As a result, African Americans will spend thousands of dollars on cars, clothing, and jewelry, because that feels and looks successful. It gives the illusion of success. Owning an expensive car purchased with money that could have been used for home ownership rarely spells success, but it looks a lot like it. With the shattered dreams of home ownership, other material things will just have to do.

It is sad that people live in a country where affirmative action is necessary. Affirmative action exposes some of our nation's existing problems. If there were no problem, laws like affirmative action would not have to be in place. The idea of landing some great corporate job because of a person's skill and education without affirmative action would be nothing more than an unrealistic dream. Much research has been done to date proving that America gives the illusion that all is fair and equal in the job market, but her citizens know different.

Anyone claiming that racism is no longer alive and well in the United States, in addition to considering the race-driven circumstances surrounding the Jena 6, or statistics demonstrating that prosecutors are far more likely to seek the death penalty when the victim is white than when the victim is black (particularly if the defendant is black), or studies demonstrating that blacks receive harsher sentences than whites for equivalent drug crimes, or the fact that even though more whites per capita smoke marihuana than blacks, blacks are

---

21 "Job Bank USA Study Shows How Deeply Black Men Face Discrimination In Hiring," by Tannette Johnson-Elie, October 8, 2003, *JSOnline - Milwaukee Journal Sentinel*, http://www.jobbankusa.com/News/Hiring/hiring100803a.html

arrested and prosecuted at a far higher rate, should read a recent study by Princeton University examining employment discrimination titled "Discrimination in Low Wage Labor Markets."[22]

This researched involved over three thousand job interviews and provided critical information in the job market. The evidence showed that a white male convict is more likely to be hired on an entry level job over a law abiding African American male.

Jobs are important because stability tremendously reduces the rate of crime. If someone feels productive with competitive wages and has somewhere to go, he or she is less likely to engage in destructive gang activity. If people have a purpose and can clearly see true advancement opportunities, allowing them to set realistic goals and pursue real world happiness, a change in the mind occurs. They go from hopeless to hopeful. If they find themselves in a rut with no true opportunity, they will become discouraged and look for unrealistic or short-lived opportunities in crime. The inward motivation is the same: money.

I have always been told that an African American has to work twice as hard for everything—even working twice as hard, most African Americans receive less income though employed in the same position on their job as others. Blacks receive less income and opportunities, and are charged higher interest rates for cars and homes. Here is an unfortunate thing: even in the year 2012, these economic issues still exist. My son just had his rude awakening going through the experiences of inequality. Different rules apply even in the good credit-bad credit scenarios regarding African Americans.

A 2005 study found that 70 percent of African Americans with incomes between $92,000 and $152,000 who bought homes were given sub-prime loans, versus 16 percent of whites in the same income range. Moreover, the NAACP claims in a lawsuit

22 "White Convicts As Likely to Be Hired As Blacks Without Criminal Records," DMIblog Politics, Policy, and the American Dream, Ezekiel Edwards, Posted at 9:09 AM, Sep 25, 2007 in Civil Rights.
Copyright 2010, Drum Major Institute for Public Policy.
http://www.dmiblog.com/archives/2007/09/white_convicts_as_likely_to_be.html

against several mortgage lenders that even when Blacks and whites were both offered sub-prime loans, African Americans were charged on average 30 percent more for the same services.[23]

Study after study in different parts of the nation are as consistent as arithmetic. They prove repeatedly that America has a major problem. Whose problem is it? Perhaps that is the question that demands an answer.

Yet another study finds that racial discrimination is alive and well in the hiring process, and it's keeping black men in metro Milwaukee on the unemployment rolls.

The study offers this fictional scenario: "A young, white, male high school graduate with a felony conviction applies in person for entry level jobs as a driver, a dishwasher, a laborer, warehouse worker and production worker that are advertised in the newspaper and admits to employers that he served 18 months in prison for possession of cocaine with intent to sell.

A young black man with similar education, work history and style of presentation, but with no criminal record, applies for the same jobs.

Who do you think is more likely to be called back?

If you picked the white man with the felony conviction, you guessed right.

This study offers evidence that discrimination remains a major factor in the economic lives of black men, and highlights the fear and misunderstanding of black males that permeate the local job market.

Devah Pager, a sociologist at Northwestern University in Evanston, Ill., sent equally matched pairs of testers—two black and two white—to apply for low-skilled jobs at 350 places of employment in the Milwaukee area and found that white ex-offenders

---

23 "Dreams Shattered in Black America"—Socialist Worker Column, by Keeanga-Yamahtta Taylor, March 15, 2010.
http://socialistworker.org/2010/03/15/dreams-shattered.

were more likely to be called back for an interview than black applicants who had no criminal record.[24]

As long as this nation continues to hide behind illusions regarding our ethnic issues, our problems with race will go unsolved. Closing our eyes will not erase, eradicate, or improve our race relations. Living in the reality and exposing these problems for the purpose of solutions is one step closer toward a better America.

---

[24] "Job Bank USA Study Shows How Deeply Black Men Face Discrimination in Hiring," by Tannette Johnson-Elie, October 8, 2003, JSOnline - Milwaukee Journal Sentinel, http://www.jobbankusa.com/News/Hiring/hiring100803a.html

CHAPTER 10

GANGSTA OR SOLDIER

America as a whole cringes when we hear the word *gangsta*. The word *gangsta* is simply a spinoff from the word gangster. In order to understand what a gangsta is, the reader must first reach back into history to discover the meaning of the word *gangster*.

Gangster movies have made millions of dollars. Many would argue that gangster movies have been the theme of choice for decades. There was the thrill of organized crime, portrayed by the mobsters or Mafia. These story lines followed the don, identified to fans as the gang's leader. With mixed emotions, many have found themselves rooting at times for the bad person and at other times the good. When the police were involved, some were corrupt, while others took a stand against violence and corruption. The viewers' hearts were bursting with shock, excitement, and suspense, not knowing who would win or what would happen next.

> Crime and Gangster Films are developed around the sinister actions of criminals or gangsters, particularly bank robbers, underworld figures, or ruthless hoodlums who operate outside the law, stealing and violently murdering their way through life. In the 1940s, a new type of crime thriller emerged, more dark and cynical …
>
> Crime stories in this genre often highlight the life of a crime figure or a crime's victim(s). Or they glorify the rise and fall of a particular criminal(s),

gang, bank robber, murderer or lawbreakers in personal power struggles or conflict with law and order figures, an underling or competitive colleague, or a rival gang. Headline-grabbing situations, real-life gangsters, or crime reports have often been used in crime films. Gangster/crime films are usually set in large, crowded cities, to provide a view of the secret world of the criminal: dark nightclubs or streets with lurid neon signs, fast cars, and piles of cash, sleazy bars, contraband, seedy living quarters or rooming houses. Exotic locales for crimes often add an element of adventure and wealth ...[25]

People mimic what they see on television and in the streets. We create our own immorality by glorifying and glamorizing wickedness on the television. In my opinion, Hollywood must take some of the blame, but not all of it. Society is bloodthirsty and hungry for violence. Hollywood simply gives its fans the movies and sitcoms that its audience will pay to see. The world as a whole loves police chases, shootouts, and aggression on every level. Gangsters brought this thrilling lifestyle of adventure to the television scene in the 1930s. However, the sad part is that most of these thrilling action scenes were taken from real-life events.

Now what about the good old gunslinging cowboys who ruled the west? Were they not bank and stagecoach robbers? Today we would call these cowboys ruthless thugs, cold- blooded killers, and gangbangers. Yet many movies portray this as an acceptable lifestyle and a rewarding way of life. How quickly we forget history, and perhaps our forgetfulness has been the moral downfall of America and even humanity.

Outlaw gangs go as far back in history as the beginning of man, with the word "thug" (Thugz) dating to 1200 A.D. when gangs in India were pillaging many of the country's towns. These gangs often had their own hand

---

25 Crime-Gangster Films, AMC Filmsite written and edited by Tim Dirks, Copyright 2010, American Movie Classics Company LLC. http://www.filmsite.org/crimefilms.html.

signs, rituals, symbols and slang, as they clustered together for means of force and protection.

During the 1800's, Americans were fascinated by gangs and their members such as the James Gang, Billy the Kid's Gang, the Doolin-Dalton Gang, the Wild Bunch and dozens of others that ruled the Wild West.

Though the history of these Old West gangs is often romanticized, it should not be forgotten that they were in fact, nothing more than thugs.[26]

Children begin playing acceptable games like cowboys and Indians. May I ask who made this game of mockery acceptable? Could Hollywood influence and set the moral standards for the world? The cowboys are good, and the Indians are the savages. Would you not agree that this message is degrading at the least? If this type of violence were acceptable and glorified then, what makes it unacceptable in the streets today? The hypocrisy of America is another problem that is destroying this nation.

Soldiers in the hood and urban areas are protectors of the streets. These soldiers are both young and old. The young are utilized as lookouts and drug delivery boys because they are too young to go to jail. The longer that these young boys and girls remain on the streets dealing in drugs, the more ruthless and hardcore they become. Their hearts become callous, as hard and cold as stone, because of the countless hours of exposure to crime. The older soldiers are the ones who give the commands. The gang or crew is the battalion or unit. Criminal activity on the streets continues to be very organized, and the bond among "boys" (close friends) is strong. They live together, work together, struggle together, eat and play together as a military unit does. These citizens exist as a city within a city, and on a larger scale, as a nation within a nation. Perhaps this struggle will never end because of the countless number of wealthy Americans behind it. A gangsta is a street soldier who is a protector of his or her community against all threats, foreign or domestic. People will see these men

---

26 Legends of America, 8926 Cedar Hill Loop, Warsaw, MO 65355.
A Travel Site for the Nostalgic & Historic Minded,
Copyright 2003–2011,
http://www.legendsofamerica.com/we-outlawgangslist.html
www.LegendsofAmerica.com.

openly flaunting signs to keep enemies away and to signify one's identity. The marking on the walls called "graffiti" is to mark out territory and to warn of impending danger.

Consider for a moment this ridiculous argument. If America glorifies gunslinging cowboys, gangsters in the mob, or the Mafia, why not glorify gangsters on the streets today? Gangstas today are no different from the gangsters that Hollywood has glorified; they too might enjoy their names going down in history like Al Capone and others. These men and women are also attempting to make a legendary fame for themselves and for their hood. Most US citizens agree that no crime on any level should ever be glorified, and we agree that criminal activity is never right.

Now let us get to the significant part. The significant part is found in the mind of little immature children. Does the glorified violence that they see violate every fiber of their God-given moral code of ethics? Of course it does, in every way and on every level of evil. Does being labeled a soldier justify gang activity? Simply put, labels neither qualify nor justify. Does labeling deceive the hearts of the naive and unsuspecting? Yes, it does. Labeling perverts the heart because it makes the good seem evil and the evil good. It is good to be a soldier in the US Army. I was, and would say that it is great to be a soldier and to defend the country in which we live. However, we cannot allow our children's minds to become mixed up, misunderstanding the difference between being a soldier in the military and being a soldier on the streets. Parents must protect their children by taking a stand. Children need a good education and a tremendous amount of positive exposure. Neighborhoods need more advertisements on television and on street corners against crime. Parents must show their children another way and a way out. Television should have less infomercials and more information about community activities, development programs, and additional educational opportunities. America needs multiracial superheroes who battle gangstas on the streets. The superhero character must mimic one that the children can identify with. The story line and subjects have to be about everyday issues that these inner-city kids constantly and consistently face. Each episode must have a good moral lesson and some kind of service announcement, which will expose the children to programs in their communities. The crime dog says, "Crime doesn't pay," but many cannot relate to this statement because crime does pay. Though the payment is short-lived with immediate consequences or gratification, the truth is that it does pay. It is not about tomorrow's payday on the streets; it is all about today's dividends. People need to show these children that, yes, crime pays, but they do not want to be the recipient of its short-lived payment and destructive lifestyle.

Children emulate what they see on television regardless of the fact that these shows might be violent or destructive. Positive imagery and role models can make a huge difference. The big brother-big sister programs are affecting communities in many positive ways. The power is in the public's hands. Parents have a major responsibility to screen what their children are watching on television and in the movie theaters. It is up to the parents, grandparents, and the public to make the difference on the streets.

CHAPTER 11

MUSIC LYRICS AND POETRY

The world loves to hear a good song or a masterful piece of poetry. Both professional artists and amatures express feelings like happiness, pain, and sorrow through poetry and music lyrics. Great artists are able to speak to the current issues of the day and past problems of yesterday that have plagued the hearts of many. Frequently, these heartfelt underlying messages are missed. People must listen intently and learn in order to relate.

The voices of the small, poor, and minority are seldom heard. These voices scream the loudest, demanding someone's attention. Yet, regardless of how loudly one may scream, it remains true that the victor is usually the one most often heard. The victor exposes what he or she has seen, heard, and felt—but from only one point of view. Many years later, often something is written that gives readers additional information exposing the error or affirming the truth. New information is brought to light, and many new facts are revealed. Oftentimes many forget that one must always consider both sides of every story to gain knowledge with accuracy and completeness.

While it is true that some lyrics have an ambiguous message, the meaning of others is clear. First, one must consider what the song or poetry meant to its composer or author. Second, consider the context to get a true understanding and the true message that is being revealed. Finally, perhaps one could ask what the lyrics or poetry mean to the individual listener.

All genres of music and messages in poetry have some kind of intent. Listen to the songs of your favorite artist. Ask yourself what the message is that this artist is attempting to convey. In the sixties, music was one thing that drove the nation. These music lyrics disclosed the heartfelt feelings and attitudes of many.

> Rock n' roll was a symbol of Black empowerment to White people, especially to racists. Many White people of the time were accustomed to and valued a separation of the races, but were now legally forced to operate against those segregationist values. The resistance to rock n' roll music, highly enjoyed by young White kids, was a culmination of all the hostility and tension of the Civil Rights movement. The resistance was manifested in two ways: some Whites used rock n' roll music as a focus-point for an open campaign of anti-Black sentiment and others excluded Blacks from public media outlets. The Ku Klux Klan and other White-supremacist organizations regained activity, openly preaching the exaggerated consequences of listening to rock n' roll music (p. 37–8). The term "jungle music" was used to describe the rock n' roll beat, declaring it would cause the White youth to lose their sense of humanity and dignity while mixing races.[27]

So many songs have reached out expressing the feeling of the day and attempted to bring a new hope for tomorrow. Selecting one song over another would prove to be tedious and exhausting. So instead, consider just a few songs that I have selected for the purpose of illustrating my point. While this book is limited in regard to complete lyrics of songs and poems because of copyright laws, the reader is encouraged to retrieve a complete copy.

The famous "We Shall Overcome" was written to encourage and strengthen the fainthearted who have found themselves involved in some sort of struggle. It was sung often during the civil rights era because of the tremendous struggles involving the African American

---

27 "Summary of *All Shook Up: How Rock N' Roll Changed America* by Glenn C. Altschuler," Associated Content from Yahoo! Inc. Yahoo News Network. http://www.associatedcontent.com/article/5440588/summary_of_all_shook_up_how_rock_n_pg 2.html?cat=37. G. C. Altschuler's *All Shook Up: How Rock 'N' Roll Changed America* was published in New York by Oxford University Press in 2003.

race against slavery, brutality, inequality, and segregation. The lyrics encourage patience and resolve, believing that by faith regardless of the struggle our day will come. Like "We Shall Overcome," "I Shall Not Be Moved" is sung in churches and at concerts, and the theme is even echoed on the streets. The song strengthens struggling souls to stand strong in God, never being moved out of one's place. It encourages victims to stand strong in the face of adversity. With a tremendous faith, the persecuted believed that the light of God would someday shine through and that we are the reflections of that light. This brings me to the song entitled "This Little Light of Mine." Slow progress was being made during the early 1920's, but slow is always better than none. Light punches holes in darkness, and if enough people in the struggle would let their lights shine, those lights would eventually overcome the darkness. These lyrics gave the oppressed a glimmer of hope in the midst of a deep, dark world. Each song or poem has been abbreviated to support the current copyright laws. I encourage each reader to look deeply into the full version of each recommended piece of literature and suggested songs.

In Sam Cooke's hit song "Change Is Gonna Come," he describes the difficulties of the civil rights era. His song speaks of the trying times of both blacks and whites. In this song, he speaks of death because of the multiple senseless killings of African Americans by whites, but he also speaks of going to his brother for help but instead is "knocked down."

> Then I go to my brother
> And I say, "Brother, help me please."
> But he winds up knocking me
> Back down on my knees.[28]

People want change, but the right kind of change. The struggle continues, but the foundation has been laid. Musical artists today are stressing and emphasizing the same need for change in many ways. There will always be a need for unity, love, and tolerance. Here are a few additional contemporary songs that stress the importance of change.

---

28 Sam Cooke's "Change Is Gonna Come" appeared on his album *The Man and His Music*.

Where Is the Love?
But we still got terrorists here livin…'
The Bloods and The Crips and the KKK.
But if you only have love for your own race,
Then you only leave space to discriminate.[29]

In 1985, Michael Jackson and Lionel Richie, with a group of great singers, came together and sang the song "We Are the World" to raise money for famine relief for Africa.

Ohhhh that a change can only come,
when we stand together as one.
We are the World, We are the children,
We are the ones who make a brighter day so let's start giving.[30]

Even Tupac Shakur, who is a hardcore rapper, cried out for change. This segment highlights some of his lyrics while leaving others out because of the explicit language. The overall message is that some people do not care about the African American and a change has to occur. "Is life worth living?" is one of many questions asked as some contemplate the idea of suicide. He refers to many clearly stated dilemmas of life. They are racism, poverty, skin color, drug abuse, and crime in the inner city. Tupac refers to the hatred of the black man by the white race, but also refers to how black people do not get along with each other. If the black man demands respect, he must first respect himself. Tupac speaks of the evils on the streets, referring to drug dealers selling drugs to children for money. He affirms that the way things were done in the past has not worked, and so there must be a change in every way. He closes his song speaking against police brutality and the brutality of revenge against one another on the streets. He, too, alludes to the evils of crime in particular black-on-black crime.

29 Black Eyed Peas, "Where Is the Love?"
http://www.azlyrics.com/lyrics/blackeyedpeas/whereisthelove.html.

30 We Are The World (Michael Jackson and Friends) Lyrics
Lyrics Artists: U Usa For Africa We Are The World (Michael Jackson and Friends)
LyricsFreak © 2013
http://www.lyricsfreak.com/u/usa+for+africa/we+are+the+world+michael+jackson+and+friends_20905699.html

First ship 'em dope & let 'em deal the brothers
give 'em guns step back watch 'em kill each other ...
I see no changes all I see is racist faces
misplaced hate makes disgrace to races"...[31]

Poets likewise wrote messages of truth, declaring the struggles in this life and hoping for a better place. The struggles in this life bring pain, fear, and loss. Yet struggles are not the end but only the beginning. The question is not will people struggle; it is what will they do with their struggles. Some have written graceful poems describing the pain and the small victories within.

Why God Made Me Black
Why do people see my skin
and think I should be abused?
Why is it some people want to hate me
and not know the person within?[32]

The famous poet Maya Angelo wrote the poem "Still I Rise."

You may write me down in history
With your bitter, twisted lies,
You may trod me in the very dirt
But still, like dust, I'll rise...[33]

Poetry is beautiful and expressive. Even amateurs like my wife Nikki and I have used poetry to express thoughts. The first poem, "In The Mirror What Do I See" and the second, "Transition of the Mind" directly relates to the title of the book.

---

31 Tupac Shakur, "Changes."
    Writer(s): Tupac Amaru Shakur
    Copyright: Universal Music Corp.
    http://www.azlyrics.com/lyrics/2pac/changes.html

32 "Why God Made Me Black," By RuNett Nia Ebo.
    Newworld GS Poetry.
    https://gspoetry.com/overmars/poems/why-god-made-me-black

33 "Still I Rise" by Maya Angelou.
    http://www.poemhunter.com/poem/still-i-rise/Maya Angelou.

In the Mirror, What Do I See?

As I look into the mirror, what do I see?
I see me.
I don't see what you want me to be.
I have dreams and want them to come true,
But how can they?
If all that you want is for me to be like you,
Not that being like you is wrong or bad,
It just doesn't fit in with the dreams that I once had.
Maybe I'll write a book to tell of my quest,
I'll put it down on paper and give it my best.
I'll tell you the truth about me,
I'll tell you everything that I wanted to be.
If you'll let me, I'll express and speak free,
I'll speak freely without a shattered dream.
But will that day ever come for me?
As I look into the mirror, what do I see?
I see a man—not black or white.
A strong man who is ready for the fight.
I don't see a slave or inferior me,
I don't even see the man that you want me to be.
I see me,
One like all made in the image of God,
His creation, a creation of God.
I see a man that exists, a man who is free,
Blessed in every way, that man is me.
When I look into the mirror, that is what I see.
God made me black, I am very proud of that.
I will not be ashamed of who I am.
For who I am is what I am,
I am a man.
I will not complain,
For this is what God wanted me to be.
As I look into the mirror, this is what I see.
And what may I ask is wrong with being me?[34]

---

34 Written by Tony D'Angelo Cloud, PhD.

Transition of the Mind

Transition of the mind
is where you want to be
to set you free
from the mentality,
from the stereotype that makes one prejudiced,
which makes one blind,
and then you find
that you cannot see
beyond the state of mind.
And so you need to find
a better way of looking at mankind,
the way Jesus broke the barrier
that holds us carriers
of hatred for another race
and you never get to know
that person you might adore.
Because inside you find
there's hatred to the core.
Jesus created a multitude of people
to love each other with an open mind
for all mankind.
When you transition the mind,
you will find
that we are all the same,
we all have pain.
Let's break the chain
and make a difference
in a world that's insane.[35]

---

35 Written by Mrs. Miriam Mekeda Cloud.

CHAPTER 12

JACK-IN-THE-BOX

Do you remember the old windup toy called a jack-in-the-box? Set to music, the box arm was manually moved in a winding circular motion, and at a set time, out popped Jack. Children have loved and played with jack-in-the-boxes for decades.

Emotionally and intellectually speaking, people put themselves into boxes. One might say that people compartmentalize their lives. Some even find themselves stuck in a rut because of their inability or refusal to expose themselves or experience things that exist outside of their comfort zones or boxes. Someone once said, "Birds of a feather flock together." This statement regarding people of like minds is true. Let's take a look at four categories of people.

Most Americans have extremely busy lives, and they find themselves going nowhere at a fast pace, spinning around in circles. The first category are people who have become trapped in the same environment; home, experiencing a mundane and redundant life held captive to social circles, job experiences, hobbies, ideas, fun, and fantasies. Jack, too, is stuck inside of a box, but it is impossible for him to get out of his box or change. This idea of change is unfortunately like pulling teeth for so many in this great society. Someone once asked the question, "Can an old dog be taught new tricks?" Unfortunately, an old dog cannot learn new tricks unless the old dog has a willingness to learn. Regrettably, for some, change is not an option, but for most, there is a world of opportunity. Those who do not possess the desire to change will remain stuck inside of an old decayed box with America's good friend Jack.

People handle change in many different ways. Some, for example, are just like a jack-in-the-box, only peeking out of their boxes for a moment just to look and stare with resentment and anger. They watch their friends having fun and enjoying their lives by finding religion or some type of self-satisfaction and a measure of contentment. They peek out and curse the world for being different from what it used to be. As times change, they refuse to change with them, adding a product of bitterness instead of good. These people remain grumpy and cynical. This pessimistic attitude proves to be destructive not just to themselves but also to everyone around them. Some time ago, there were old movies where these types of people sat on their porches all day acting as grumpy as could be. The power of words gives them their strength because they use negative words. They use derogatory words and behavior from the old days, attempting to stir up hatred, strife, and violence. These people are constantly irritated, wishing for the "good old days," where things can go back to what they use to be; these people remain stuck in time, never desiring to evolve as the rest of the world slowly passes them by. Like Jack, this group of people peeks out, but the next generation forces them back into their boxes.

The next category is people who peek out of their boxes, climb out with a great effort, but then go back in. The world appreciates the fact that at least they attempted to create positive change in their lives, but they prove to lack endurance as they experience difficulty fitting in and struggle to learn new things. As the ever-so-changing world grows in population, inventions, and ideas, people have to force themselves to some degree or another to cope with it and to grow in a positive direction. What types of struggles has each generation faced as they were forced to deal with new inventions being introduced? What did people really think of Alexander Graham Bell as he worked on his new technology for communication? To most, was Alexander the crazy man next door? Was he that different and wasting his time? After all, who wanted to speak into some device when they could just go down the street to visit with friends and neighbors? If Alexander and a few of his adversaries were alive today to see where his small invention has crossed the globe and has impacted practically every person on the entire face of the earth, what would they think of him now? Technology moves at a fast pace, and sometimes it moves so fast that it can be quite intimidating, forcing some right back into their boxes. Does America forget about these struggling human beings, or does she create opportunities to help them along? Their wisdom, too, is necessary and needed for our survival. This country must find a way to keep this type of people out of their boxes. For far too long, the public has pushed the older generation aside without concern for their well-being. They are dying, and their wisdom, knowledge, and skills are dying with them. History repeats itself. In order to get ahead and to move positively toward the future, humanity must take a good honest look at history and learn from past mistakes.

The third category is gangsters. Gangsters and gangbangers, for the most part, are those who peek out of their boxes having a strong desire to get out, but struggle because their world has revolved around hopelessness for so long. Some of these people have told themselves that there is no hope, and they have forced themselves to believe that it is impossible for them to handle the requirements involved in change. The shame of starting at the bottom and making pennies compared to thousands of dollars in drug money—or the fear of their lack of knowledge—holds them back. They have lost their spirit of adventure. These people have damaged their own psyche, living inside of rooms with padded walls. Their conscience bothers them daily, and they become imprisoned in their own minds. They desperately want out, but at times are in so deeply that they have lost their sense of caring. They have lost the feeling of being loved and the feeling of loving others. The life of a gangsta is a lifestyle that no one involved in can win. The gangsta knows that one day it will end by his imprisonment or death, never knowing how, just anticipating the when. He knows that one day his fate will come. Filled with excuses and rarely finding success, casting the blame on others like a broken record or a spinning top that goes around and around, eventually his life will come to a gruesome end. The gangbanger's jack-in-the-box is out of order. It is a broken toy, being wound with a wrecked Jack who never pops out.

America as a whole can change! The thought of change is key in the fourth category. Thankfully, some peek out, get out, and stay out of their boxes. Like me, these people who are set free from their boxes welcome positive change and have become active members of a new society, effecting positive change. These people have transformed their minds with optimistic thinking. These people refuse to accept defeat as an answer and transform negative words into positive ones. They have not believed the lie they were told many years ago. The code does not work in this arena and has become a useless tool. The lack of love found inside of an empty house and the absent parental guidance inspire them to behave differently toward their offspring. Respect is something that they learn must be earned. Crime is committed against them, not by them. Holding them down or back is not an option because they see life clearly, because they have first learned to look deep inside of themselves before looking at others. These people have learned other ways to protect their family, community, and country by using their minds and gaining knowledge. Music lyrics and poetry are used as a positive force to help broaden their horizon and to take them to places they have never gone before. The useless proverbial phrase "You can take the boy out of the hood, but you can't take the hood out of the boy" is eliminated. They have the keys to their destiny and are in complete control of their lives. They have eliminated their box of shame.

There are many good examples of people who have risen out of poverty, crime, and gang-infested neighborhoods. There are good people who have transformed their lives by staying out of the box of shame.

> Tyler Perry was born in New Orleans, Louisiana, on September 13, 1969. He was a middle child, with two older sisters and a younger brother. According to Margena A. Christian in *Jet,* "He says that he endured years of abuse as a child by his father 'whose answer to everything was to beat it out of you.' Perry says he would 'go places in his mind' following beatings." At one point, unable to take it anymore Perry attempted to kill himself, slashing his wrists in an action that he has called a cry for attention. "I was pretty young and totally frustrated," he told Christian.[36]

Another good example is Mr. T, a Hollywood movie star from the A-Team.

> Laurence Tureaud had grown up on Chicago's South Side in the Robert Taylor Homes, home then to the

36 Encyclopedia of World Biography, Tyler Perry Biography.
   http://www.notablebiographies.com/newsmakers2/2006-Le-Ra/Perry-Tyler.
   html#ixzz1bFQ5jFIH.

largest concentration of poverty in America. Degraded housing stock, high levels of environmental pollutants, and the residents' lack of money and inadequate access to healthcare had turned this space and other public housing projects across urban America into asthma zones. In the projects of Chicago, African Americans were almost five times more likely to die of asthma than whites ...[37]

While growing up Tureaud regularly witnessed murder, rape, and other crimes, but attributes his survival and later success to his will to do well and his mother's love.[38]

Perhaps if we took the time to seriously think about it, we could name many actors, actresses, friends, family, and perhaps ourselves as people who have overcome great obstacles. Stories about people's lives from rags to riches almost always touch the human heart. Many of these amazing stories involve people having been addicted to drugs and alcohol and some suffering from domestic issues and sexual abuse. Knowing someone who has overcome gives others hope, and hope is a great feeling.

Coolio, for example, couldn't read until he was twelve years old. Jimmy Hendrix was born in poverty and often neglected. An amazing and impressive story is the one about Chris Gardner. His life was depicted in the movie *The Pursuit of Happyness*, starring Will Smith. He basically lost everything trying to make a better life for himself and his family. What about the many great musicians and actors who were given a chance and completely turned their lives around? Shawn "Jay-Z" Carter, though from the hood, is worth millions today. Take a look at the projects in America. Now take a second look at them in the sixties. The conditions were horrific. In spite of these terrible conditions, many still made it to the top. Muhammad Ali, a man who was born and lived in these conditions, is another great example. His

---

37 "A Place-Based Malady: How We Help Create Our Allergic Landscape," by Gregg Mitman. Published in the May/June 2007 issue of *Orion* magazine, 187 Main Street, Great Barrington, MA 01230, 413-528-4422. http://www.orionmagazine. org/index.php/articles/article/274/.

38 From Wikipedia, the free encyclopedia, http://en.wikipedia.org/wiki/Mr._T#cite_ ref-mrt40_3-0, en.wikipedia.org/wiki/Mr._T.

powerful influence remains and will probably continue to positively affect mankind until the world as we know it is no more. I guess that my point is, if they can do it, so can everyone else. We should never give up on life.

Life is an uncertain journey that we all go on. There are many battles and struggles, and one might even say that life is full of great and tremendous conflicts. These conflicts bring ever before us, deep valleys and high mountains to climb. For thousands of years, many of God's people have felt as though we are fighting a battle that we just can't win. As a result, many brethren have given up, believing that we just can't do it.

Here is a great question for today. How much is your soul worth to you? Perhaps that is the major and most important theme of life: our souls.

Pitfalls in life will come. Trials and tribulations seem to always knock at our doors. Yet God is able to rescue His people from the trials, tribulations, and temptations that would ever cause us to give up. In view of the unparalleled supremacy of God, He has rendered our excuses powerless. "If He rescued righteous Lot ... then the Lord knows how to rescue the godly from temptation ..." (2 Peter 2:7, 9).

Troubled times that come our way are from our adversary, the Devil, and are a direct result of the wickedness and weakness of humanity. The Bible says:

> We are afflicted in every way, but not crushed; perplexed, but not despairing; persecuted, but not forsaken; struck down but not destroyed; always carrying about in the body the dying of Jesus, that the life of Jesus may be manifested in our body (2 Cor. 4:7–9).
>
> Consider it all joy, my brethren, when you encounter various trials, knowing that the testing of your faith produces endurance. And let endurance have its perfect result, that you may be perfect and complete, lacking in nothing (James 1:2–4).
>
> No temptation has overtaken you but such as is common to man; and God is faithful, who will not allow you to be tempted beyond what you are able, but with the temptation will provide the way of escape also, that you may be able to endure it (1 Cor. 10:13).

Regardless of the rumors and lies that we have heard in times past, believe that we can and we will because of Jesus. who is a shelter in the time of storm. We echo the words of the Sixty-First Psalm verse two, "Lead me to the Rock that is higher than I." Lead me to Jesus, our great shepherd who restores our souls. And as Psalm 23:4 says, "Even though I walk through the valley of the shadow of death, I fear no evil; for Thou art with me; Thy rod and Thy staff, they comfort me."

God made us in His image, which tells me that He made us great people from all walks of life. Through our trusting faith, hard determination, and positive thinking, we can and we will. God came to give us an abundant life.

CHAPTER 13

A FEW IDEAS

How can this nation help solve the problem of gang violence? The problem itself can never be resolved because of the wickedness of the human heart. However, it can be dramatically decreased if the entire nation takes a positive stand and gets involved. Citizens cannot be so naive as to believe that a national effort will ever come to pass, but on the other hand, we can be optimistic enough to believe that we can make a positive change that can be felt in cities and communities that want to get involved.

For far too long, action against gang violence has been reactive. By the time our law enforcement comes to the crime scene, it is usually far too late. It is like having a problem with an infestation of termites: once the insects are discovered, there are thousands in existence, and to destroy them drastic measures must be taken. The problem with drastic measures is that the police then must enter into a neighborhood and arrest everyone—the good, bad, innocent, and guilty. That is the problem with being reactive instead of proactive. This approach has destroyed the relationships and trust that people in these neighborhoods once had for officers of the law. Being reactive has permitted the bulk of communities to be infested and to get way out of control. The reaction time of humans has proven to be too slow; citizens of this great country must take a proactive approach. The problem of infestation can be solved by being both proactive and consistent. I am proposing an approach for people to consider that will prove to be more economically feasible and will involve everyone in one way or another.

Having a proactive approach is nothing new. People are proactive in the sports draft, business decisions, politics, marriage relationships, insurance, and the list goes on; why not take a proactive stand against gang violence? Who in any given neighborhood does not know when gangs are moving into their community or territory? Perhaps there are some who are naive and oblivious to the problem. Some states have tried neighborhood watch, but what is actually needed is neighborhood action. Gang leaders are usually wise enough to know when they are up against a losing battle, and they tend to move on. It is easier and more desirable for gangs to go where there is the least amount of resistance because they have a reputation on the streets to uphold. It will take many government entities and every community member to ensure the success of this program. We need justice! Everyone must have their eyes open, writing down license plate numbers and reporting them to the proper authorities. Churches have the ability to produce many great rehabilitation programs and to organize great community intervention. The police must respond rapidly and in force, immediately taking action and demanding respect in all communities, not just in the suburbs or upper-class neighborhoods. Officers can use nonviolent force and continually encourage open communication with gangbangers. Show and treat gangbangers with adequate respect, and they will return that respect to you. Someone has to be the leader in taking the high road. Talk to these gang members and remind them of the fact that a life of violence ends brutally and quickly. Seek out the weak and start to dissolve the gang by giving the weaker members opportunities to change. The weak are followers and far easier to persuade. People as a whole do not aspire to be in gangs, and most are looking for an opportunity and a way out. Gangs are dramatically weakened when their members are in the wings secretly waiting for their chance and an opportunity to change.

Loitering after curfews must become a crime punishable by jail time, community service, and fines. If gangs have nowhere to congregate, a community removes the opportunity for their neighborhood to be designated as a territory. An animal marks its territory, and humans do likewise. An example of territorial markings is the gang colors of the Bloods and the Crips. Removing the opportunity to mark a territory makes the land a neutral zone. In other words, do not give gangs a meeting place in any of your neighborhoods.

Make strong embarrassing examples of violators. Be fair and

honest, but firm. Community service is an unpleasant feeling for a gangbanger. It is worse than jail. Public community service destroys a thug's reputation quickly. The community service has to be displayed as a public service seen by all. The truth of the matter is that thugs cannot be seen helping society. Allow community service jobs to teach a skill, being used to train the youth and to give them the rewarding feeling of hard work and success. Force these youths to earn their freedom from community service, making freedom a precious and valuable commodity to them. The punishment cannot be enjoyable; it has to have a positive mental and emotional effect on the recipient. Make community service occur around the time that most gang activity has been taking place in the communities. Take away their Friday and Saturday nights with jobs that are labor-intensive and exhausting. In addition, there must be individual counseling for true rehabilitation to occur. I am sure that your local churches will offer free counseling to their members.

Exposure to new environments is a worthwhile effort. Exposure to positive programs and real opportunities also proves to be valuable. Add care centers that teach trades, art, technology, language, finance, military, entrepreneur opportunities, and music to high school students, giving them a jump-start along with some additional guidance and direction. Stimulate a level of hope in their hearts and increase their desire to succeed. Get them out of their communities on field trips, exposing them to new things and introducing them to numerous lifestyles. There are many successful retired residents who are looking for opportunities to give back to their communities. Their help is valuable and necessary.

The Boys and Girls Clubs of America are needed in every community, as well as the YMCA. These well-organized community centers have proven their worth over many years. There are programs that are designed to help all youth, but their existence is not always well-publicized. Perhaps the advertising is poor because of funding. Programs, like anything else, will have less success if the community does not know they exist.

For the most part, children just need a positive, constructive place to go and good role models to follow. Offer opportunities to successful older men and women who grew up in their community to speak to these youths and to encourage their parents. Allow them to tell about their mistakes and struggles, but also success and reality.

Teach multiculturalism and encourage leadership. Older men and women from their communities speaking to inner-city youths show longevity of life and prove to these children that they do not have to die young. While many have shortened their days here on earth, remind children that this does not have to be them. There are many safe and constructive places for youths to go in their own communities today. There are boxing gyms, after-school programs, church programs, military programs, martial arts, 4-H, dance, various foundations, athletic programs—and even a job is not a bad way to go. There are mentoring programs like Big Brothers Big Sisters and athletic mentoring or coaching programs.

Encourage children to see and interact with police officers, both in and out of uniform. This will show that police officers are real people with families and friends. In addition, it will give young people the opportunity to see police officers and their dogs as friendly and helpful, instead of as the enemy. Law enforcement needs to build trust and prove to the younger generation that not all police officers are corrupt. While some officers are violators of the law, most are law-abiding citizens. Their image in the eyes of the younger generation needs to be seen in a more positive light. A police officer in Maryland named Ronny took me out on a ride-along, and it has tremendously influenced my life to this day.

Jails and prisons are necessary and can be very helpful. Prisoners should have to grow their own foods and work eight to twelve hours daily six days a week. The work that they do should be something that benefits both the prison and the community. Skill-building opportunities must be earned through hard work and trust. In other words, opportunities for rehabilitation must be offered. There should be jobs in agriculture created for prisoners. The prison should grow and raise its own food, both for sale and for the inmates' daily rations. The inmate should be informed on how the job or jobs that they are participating in help the community and the prison, which can build morality, confidence, and self-worth. Each inmate should be paid from the profit earned by the prison and community. This money will first fund the prison, then the community, and last, the inmate's personal account. The inmates will receive their money upon release from incarceration so that they are not placed back on the streets with no funds. The hardest thing for an ex-convict to get upon his or her release is a stable job. Without a stable job or money, many chose a life of crime for survival purposes. Money and a skill could reduce the number of repeat offenders on the streets.

Each gangbanging criminal must earn his or her freedom within the prison system. Inmates should be shipped to prisons that are outside of their comfort zones, which will give them exposure to a new way of life. For example, inmates who are born and raised in the city should be shipped to quiet country prisons. Inmates from cold climates should be moved to hotter climates and vice versa. By removing the inmate from his territory or gang, he or she will lose communication with prior associates. The streets evolve like computers, so it will not take long for this individual to lose power, fame, and respect on the streets. Upon returning to the streets, the inmates' reputations will be tarnished, forcing or giving the opportunity for change.

There can be no free rides within the system. Free meals, free medical care, and rewards for bad behavior must end. Everything, including toiletries, must be earned or purchased. It becomes a privilege to have material gain and gives the feeling of success on every level. The rules must be clearly visible and must equally apply to each person. Inmates caught stealing, fighting, or breaking any rules mandated by the warden will be punished and lose everything, including their mattresses but excluding their sheets for warmth. Prison should never be comfortable, pleasurable, or painless. A prison system and schedule that is filled with hard work will force the inmates to live with each other in a civilized way; they will begin to develop good habits of tolerance and good, strong work ethics. Make each inmate accountable! Most of these inmates will think twice about returning. One of the most important rules for this system has to be respect. The inmates must respect authority, each other, and themselves. In addition, the prison staff must do likewise respecting inmates in the same way.

Find things that each prisoner aspired at one time in their hearts to become and offer them self-education opportunities by ordering textbooks within that industry. Increase their feeling of hope and productivity, assuring them that one day they will get a second chance.

Give lifers the opportunity to earn better living conditions than the rest by becoming role models and good examples. They should be given an opportunity to pay back to society the debt that they now owe. Create non-release restitution programs within each prison. Though they acted in society like animals, they will not be treated as animals if they choose not to be and are willing to show respect and follow the rules. Allow them the opportunity to earn things in this program that are confined to their rooms, luxuries that they would not want to give up. I am proposing that these inmates be made to feel proud, productive, responsible, appreciated, and respected adults. This will decrease their stress load and discourage their motivation to dominate others. Since lifers have nothing to lose, give them something to gain. For those who do not comply, permanent isolation is the only real answer. Bad company corrupts good morals. Segregate inmates who have no desire to rehabilitate to ensure the success of these strategies.

This world is always only one generation away from a complete change, whether good or bad. The children are our future. Protect the children and expose them to better things, and they will begin to dream. Most of the human race has given up in so many ways. The entire human race can change and be held to a higher standard. The world can experience change one person at a time, you should be that one person it starts with.

CHAPTER 14

RACISM AND POLITICS IN AMERICA

A tragedy that humans face is racism. One of the most serious results of racism is division. Division has destroyed and will destroy many nations. Jesus said, "Every kingdom divided against itself is brought to desolation; and every city or house divided against itself shall not stand" (Matt. 12:25). Racism has haunted the entire world ceaselessly. It is a product of humans' inability to both compromise and be unbiased in thought. Humanity is very intolerant of each other. Racism is the inclination to judge a person based on his skin pigmentation or ethnic background. Far too many people struggle with racist minds. These minds have the seeds of hate and pride sown into them. The Word of God teaches that all human beings are created in the image of God. Therefore, all people are equal in the sight of God, with differences of gender and talent that are no basis for prejudicial judgment.

Racism has been a part of America's past and present. Many American citizens are racist. They have attempted to disguise their racism. How do they disguise racism? Churches have been used in so many ways. Some church leaders speak of one God for all, but in many cases practice the opposite. For example,

> A small eastern Kentucky church is making huge headlines after it banned interracial couples from becoming members. The decision comes after a current member of Gulnare Free Will Baptist Church in Pikeville became engaged to a man from South Africa.

Coming home from college for the holidays, Stella Harville and her fiancé, Ticha Chikuni, brought news of their engagement to her church family.[39]

A fear remains about the increase of multiracial couples. Here we are in the year 2013, and the ugly seed of racism is still present. Even some church outreach programs are limited by race.

Corporate America disguises racism through affirmative action, hiring the minimum number of minorities necessary. If Caucasians show extreme kindness to minorities, they too are secretly treated inhumanly by their own race. Some older African Americans remain angry with some Caucasians in America because of the past inhumane treatment of the African American race.

The 2010 Census report stated that 72.4 percent of America's population is Caucasian and 12.6 percent African American. Some media reports display crime as an African American problem. The racist Americans seek to justify their actions. One justification is through the phrase "Things have always been this way." Judicially speaking, there are old laws that have not been revised since the days of segregation. Racism is a powerful evil. It denies all people the opportunity to share fellowship, though they may possess common interests. Racism refuses to go away for many reasons. One of those reasons is the feelings of superiority still existing among certain groups. These teachings influence the hearts and minds of our youth in a negative way. Economics is another reason that racism strongly remains in force. A part of corporate America still refuses to pay African Americans what they are worth. Some do not have a desire for African Americans to advance even to this day. All men and women with the same credentials should be paid the same amount and have the same opportunities.

Racism in America has even influenced the outcome of political policies and rules. The forty-fourth president of America is an African American. This African American president is a good illustration regarding America's race issues. His father is a black man from Kenya and his mother a white woman from Kansas. He is 50 percent black

39 Hearst Television Inc., Internetbroadcasting CNN, Hearst Properties Inc. on behalf of WLKY. By Ann Bowdan/WLKY, Posted: 5:11 pm EST December 1, 2011, Updated: 8:20 am EST December 2, 2011, http://www.wlky.com/news/29901119/detail.html#ixzz1fQkYe2gC.

and 50 percent white, but that appears to be too much black for some in America. It is an American's right to have different political views. The Democrats want the Republicans out, and the Republicans want the Democrats out. The political parties continually work against each other. Both Democrats and Republicans want to be in office and share a desire to rule our nation. The racist issues spoken of here are not to be confused with the normal political issues that we have for years been bombarded with. In areas strictly associated with racism, political intolerance involving America's African American president is on display.

This presidential administration has provided many occasions for this country to raise the issues of race. Here are a few examples.

> An email sent by Marilyn Davenport, an elected member of the Orange County Republican party, that features the face of President Obama superimposed on a chimpanzee.... The email depicts Obama as a chimpanzee with two older chimpanzee "parents." Superimposed on the digitally altered image? "Now you know why – No birth certificate!"[40]

> The so-called birther movement began during the 2008 campaign when some of Barack Obama's critics claimed, without offering proof, that he was born in Kenya, like his father, Barack Obama Sr. The Constitution clearly states that no one born in another country is eligible to become president. So, this tactic was used to eliminate him.
>
> During the 2008 campaign, two fact-checking groups, FactCheck.org and PolitiFact, had concluded the certification of live birth was authentic. But the issue remained potent among conservative voters. In April 2011, a New York Times-CBS News poll found that a plurality of Republican voters, 47 percent, said they believed Mr. Obama was born in another country; 22 percent said they did not know where he was born,

---

40 "California Politician's Email Depicts Obama as a Chimp, Sparks Outrage," by Nick Gass, April 18, 2011, ABC News. http://abcnews.go.com/Politics/marilyn-davenport-chimp-email-ignites-controversy-republicans/story?id=13400480.

and 32 percent said they believed he was born in the United States.[41]

New York Times columnist Timothy Egan explained that the birther movement "has little to do with reality and everything to do with the strangeness of Obama's background—especially his race." He continued, "Many Republicans refuse to accept that Obama could come from such an exotic stew and still be 'American.' ... So, even though the certificate of live birth first made public in 2008 is a legal document that any court would have to recognize, they demanded more."[42]

The "Tea Party" has been accused of having a partly racist agenda. At rallies across America, signs have been posted and hand carried with many racial undertones. The political leaders and spokesmen at these rallies have disregarded these racist signs. These signs are unnecessary if the problem is political, but the problem is more than political, it is both political and racial. "Tea Party" leader Mark Williams appeared on a CNN panel on "Anderson Cooper 360" last night and promptly set to work discrediting himself and his movement. Williams denounced those carrying blatantly racist signs against President Obama during the tea parties as "no more part of the mainstream of America than the hippies who wear nipple clips and feather boas in San Francisco streets during so-called peace demonstrations." Cooper had done his homework, however, and caught Williams blatantly misrepresenting himself: "What you're saying makes sense to me here when I'm hearing what you say but then I read on your blog, you say, you call the President an Indonesian Muslim turned welfare thug and a racist in chief." Williams shrugs and responds,

41 The *New York Times*, Monday, October 24, 2011. Birther Movement (Obama Birth Certificate). http://racerelations.about.com/od/trailblazers/a/Three-Of-The-Most-Racist-Anti-Obama-Political-Attacks.htm

42 "Three of the Most Racist Anti-Obama Political Attacks," by Nadra Kareem Nittle, About.com Guide, Oct 21 2011. http://racerelations.about.com/od/trailblazers/a/Three-Of-The-Most-Racist-Anti-Obama-Political-Attacks.htm

"Yeah, that's the way he's behaving." An incredulous Cooper asks Williams if he really believes Obama is an Indonesian Muslim and a welfare thug. The tea party leader digs the hole a little deeper: "He's certainly acting like it. Until he embraces the whole country what else can I conclude."[43]

While discussing President Barack Obama and the problems involving the debt ceiling, Rep. Doug Lamborn (R-CO) made the comment that "Even if some people say, 'Well the Republicans should have done this or they should have done that,' they will hold the President responsible. Now, I don't even want to have to be associated with him [the President]. It's like touching a tar baby and you get it, you're stuck, and you're a part of the problem now and you can't get away." Realizing what he had done or being informed of it by someone, the Huffingtonpost.com reported that Lamborn tried to correct his error: "On Monday, Lamborn sent a personal letter to President Obama 'apologizing for using a term some find insensitive,'" his office said in a press release. The congressman was "attempting to tell a radio audience last week that the president's policies have created an economic quagmire for the nation and are responsible for the dismal economic conditions our country faces." Lamborn's apology to President Obama was for his use of the term "tar baby." The origin of the term comes from an Uncle Remus Br'er Rabbit story based on African folklore. However, other references to the term has been viewed as derogatory and used to represent African Americans or dark skinned people ...[44]

---

43 "'Tea Party' Leader Melts Down on CNN: Obama Is an 'Indonesian Muslim Turned Welfare Thug' (VIDEO)," Huffington Post. Nicholas Graham first posted: 09-15-09 09:02 AM; Updated: 11-15-09. http://www.huffingtonpost.com/2009/09/15/tea-party-leader-melts-do_n_286933.html.

44 "Lamborn Apologizes to Obama for Tar Baby Reference," by Paul R. Lehman August 7, 2011. http://americasraceproblem.wordpress.com/?s=Lamborn+apologizes+to+Obama+for+tar+baby.

Like biting into a rotten apple, this evil of racism has been publicly and nationally exposed.

Has America's presidential election awakened the racial issues? There was a time in America when racism was unrestrained, but such unrestraint has decreased with time. The grotesque racial crimes of the past were unchallenged, overlooked, and acceptable. The old attitudes of the South have proven to be harmful and inhumane. There are several examples of these racially motivated hate crimes in the 1930s fifties, and sixties.

In the last decades of the nineteenth century, the lynching of Black people in the Southern and border states became an institutionalized method used by whites to terrorize Blacks and maintain white supremacy. In the South, during the period 1880 to 1940, there was deep-seated and all-pervading hatred and fear of the Negro, which led white mobs to turn to "lynch law" as a means of social control. Lynchings—open public murders of individuals suspected of crime conceived and carried out more or less spontaneously by a mob—seem to have been an American invention. In *Lynch-Law*, the first scholarly investigation of lynching, written in 1905, author James E. Cutler stated that lynching is a criminal practice which is peculiar to the United States.

Most of the lynchings were by hanging or shooting, or both. However, many were of a more hideous nature—burning at the stake, maiming, dismemberment, castration, and other brutal methods of physical torture. Lynching therefore was a cruel combination of racism and sadism, which was utilized primarily to sustain the caste system in the South. Many white people believed that Negroes could only be controlled by fear. To them, lynching was seen as the most effective means of control.

There are three major sources of lynching statistics. None cover the complete history of lynching in America. Prior to 1882, no reliable statistics of lynchings were recorded. In that year, the *Chicago Tribune* first began to take systematic account of lynchings. Shortly thereafter, in 1892, Tuskegee Institute began to make a systematic collection and tabulation of lynching statistics. Beginning in 1912, the National Association for the Advancement of Colored People kept an independent record of lynching's.[45]

The "deliberate speed" called for in the Supreme Court's *Brown* decision was quickly overshadowed by events outside the nation's courtrooms. In Montgomery, Alabama, a grassroots revolt against segregated public transportation inspired a multitude of similar protests and boycotts. A number of school districts in the Southern and border states desegregated peacefully. Elsewhere, white resistance to school desegregation resulted in open defiance and violent confrontations, requiring the use of federal troops in Little Rock, Arkansas, in 1957. Efforts to end segregation in Southern colleges were also marred by obstinate refusals to welcome African Americans into previously all-white student bodies ...

On December 1, 1955, Rosa Parks, forty-three, was arrested for disorderly conducted for refusing to give up her bus seat to a white passenger ...

Seventeen African American students were selected to attend the all white Central High School in 1957 but by opening day the number had dwindled to nine. Pictured here with Daisy Bates, a newspaper journalist and active member in the local NAACP, are nine students, Ernest Green, Thelma Mothershed, Elizabeth Eckford, Terrace Roberts, Carlotta Walls, Gloria Ray, Jefferson Thomas, Melba Pattillo, and Minnijean Brown. Bates would become the advisor for the nine students. The day before school opened, Governor Orval Faubus called the National Guard to

---

45 "The Negro Holocaust: Lynching and Race Riots in the United States,1880–1950," by Robert A. Gibson, Yale-New Haven Teachers Institute. http://yale.edu/ynhti/ curriculum/units/1979/2/79.02.04.x.html#b.

surround Central High, declaring "blood would run in the streets" if blacks students attempted to enter ...[46]

Emmett Till, a black boy from a Chicago, was visiting his grandfather and grand-uncle Mose Wright in the town of Money, Mississippi, population about 360. Although warned by his mother not to talk to whites, he disregarded that warning, saying "Bye, baby" to Carolyn Bryant, a white woman working at Bryant's Grocery and Meat Market. Till and his cousin, Curtis Jones, were told to leave town. They did not. One week later, J. W. Milam and his half-brother Roy Bryant arrived at Wright's house, and abducted the "nigger here from Chicago." They beat him to death, gouging out one of his eyes, and dumped his weighted body into the Tallahatchee River. An all-white jury found the two not guilty.[47]

In the summer of 1964, three major civil rights groups united to form the Council of Federal Organizations (COFO), dedicated to promoting equality for blacks in America. COFO organized a project called Freedom Summer that aimed to help register blacks to vote in Mississippi, one of the most oppressive states for African-Americans.

Hundreds of civil rights activists, black and white, traveled to Mississippi to take part in the project. Thousands of blacks registered to vote with great enthusiasm, while local whites reacted with anti-black violence across the state. Local police and Ku Klux Klan members harassed civil rights activists, trying to quell their determination.

On June 21, 1964, three Congress of Racial Equality (CORE) activists went missing: 24-year-old Michael Schwerner and 20-year-old Andrew Goodman, both Jewish volunteers from New York, and 21-year-old

---

46 "With an Even Hand, Brown V. Board at Fifty, The Aftermath," Exhibition of the Library of Congress, July 23, 2010. http://www.loc.gov/exhibits/brown/brown-aftermath.html.

47 NNDB, "Tracking the Entire World," Soylent Communications, 2011. http://www.nndb.com/people/263/000073044/.

James Chaney, an African-American from Meridian, Miss. The three men had been arrested for speeding by Neshoba County Deputy Sheriff Cecil Price, who detained them until 10:30 p.m. and then ordered them to leave the county.

Their disappearance became national news. The CORE campaign suspected foul play and the FBI launched an investigation. It searched the area and found at least eight bodies of blacks who had been lynched, but no white bodies. It finally got a break in the case when it received a tip from a local white who was motivated by the FBI's $25,000 for information.

On Aug. 4, the FBI discovered the bodies of Schwerner, Goodman and Chaney buried deep inside an earthen well. Schwerner and Goodman had each been shot in the heart. Chaney had been badly beaten and shot three times; "I have never witnessed bones so severely shattered," said a doctor who examined Chaney's body.

The story horrified the American public and alerted it to the level of oppression that existed in the South. The civil rights movement received greater media coverage and support in the wake of the murders.[48]

"Yet the Ku Klux Klan, America's oldest terrorist organization, has never gone away. More importantly, it has never stopped trying to create terror. With eight major groups and around 40 minor ones, comprising roughly 110 chapters or "Klaverns," Klan groups are still the most common type of hate group in the United States. An estimated 4,000 to 5,000 Klan members, with greater numbers of associates, sympathizers, and those hanging on, perpetuate its history. Every year, people associated with Ku Klux Klan groups commit crimes ranging from minor acts of intimidation to major hate crimes and even terrorism. Perhaps because

---

48   "On This Day: Bodies of Three Civil Rights Workers Discovered in Mississippiby findingDulcinea Staff, August 04, 2011Dulcinea Media, Inc. http://www.findingdulcinea.com/news/on-this-day/July-August-08/On-this-Day--Bodies-of-Three-Civil-Rights-Workers-Discovered-in-Mississippi.html.

the Klan is universally familiar, Americans are apt to ignore or even to laugh at it, yet to underestimate the hatred inherent in the Klan's ideology and the violent and criminal acts that this ideology so often motivates its adherents to commit, is to make a serious error..."

Today's splintered Klan encompasses a range of beliefs. While the ideology is categorized here into religious, political, racial, and anti-Semitic beliefs for the sake of clarity, Klan members do not necessarily make the same categorical distinctions.

Klan ideology, at its core, is centered on the idea that white Americans are threatened by nonwhite minorities and that most of these threats are arranged or encouraged by a sinister Jewish conspiracy. The Klan promotes itself as a way for white Americans to right these perceived wrongs, protect themselves, and strike back at their enemies. At the heart of Klan beliefs is the notion that violence is justified in order to protect white America (Chalmers, 1987) ...

The typical Klan activist believes that African Americans are the cause of most crime in America. They also believe that blacks are intellectually inferior and have no moral sense, that they rely on welfare to survive, that they are drug users, and that black men are pathological rapists of white women. In other words, blacks are the focal point of lower- and working-class white fears ...

According to the Klan, because blacks are so unintelligent and lazy, they are incapable of accomplishing any real task or even getting a job. If any African American does hold a worthwhile or important job, therefore, it was obviously the result of affirmative action and cost a hard working "real" (i.e., white) American his or her job. This is a key part of the Klan sense of victimization, especially its belief that white males are the "real" victims. It also scapegoats blacks, allowing them to be blamed for economic failures that whites themselves experience ...

C. Edward Foster (1997) wrote that ...

> The Pennsylvania Ku Klux Klan recognizes the simple fact that ALL African niggers are all savage, bloodthirsty Satanic beasts ... In the last 30 years these cannibalistic apes have fiendishly MURDERED over 50,000 White Christians. A nigger cannot be a Christian. Voodoo is the only appropriate religion for these depraved, demonic, vile, ape-like creatures of jungle darkness. (p. 2)
> This sort of rhetoric attempts to dehumanize African Americans, to make them easier and more acceptable targets for violence and intimidation."[49]

Today these crimes are challenged and punishable. The evolving attitudes of the South have proven to be better because things have become more diversified. It was not so much diversification by choice, but over time the South has been forced into a corner. Multiracial couples have become more prevalent. As a result, multiracial children are on the rise, putting an end to any pure race.

> About two million American children have parents of different races. In the United States, marriages between blacks and whites increased 400 percent in the last 30 years, with a 1000 percent increase in marriages between whites and Asians. In a recent survey, 47% of white teens, 60% of black teens, and 90% of Hispanic teens said they had dated someone of another race.[50]

---

49 "The Ku Klux Klan: America's Forgotten Terrorists," by J. Keith Akins, PhD, Department of Criminal Justice, New Mexico State University, Law Enforcement Executive Forum, 2006, 5(7) pg. 127–133.
    J. Keith Akins, PhD, Department of Criminal Justice, New Mexico State University Learning Ace
    http://www.learningace.com/doc/581434/7d94833e9107fc18ce20a313dd51e700/kkkamericasforgottenterrorists

50 "Facts for Families, Multiracial Children,"The American Academy of Child and Adolescent Psychiatry (AACAP), 2010. No. 71; March 2011. http://www.aacap.org/cs/root/facts_for_families/multiracial_children.

The populations are shifting, weakening the once-dominant Caucasian race.

The race and Hispanic-origin 2 distribution of the U.S. population is projected to become more diverse. As the Black; Asian and Pacific Islander; American Indian, Eskimo, and Aleut; and Hispanic-origin populations increase their proportions of the total population, the non-Hispanic White population proportion would decrease. By the turn of the century, the non-Hispanic White proportion of the population is projected to decrease to less than 72 percent with about 13 percent Black; 11 percent Hispanic origin; 4 percent Asian and Pacific Islander; and less than 1 percent American Indian, Eskimo, and Aleut. By 2050, the proportional shares shift quite dramatically. Less than 53 percent would be non-Hispanic White; 16 percent would be Black; 23 percent would be Hispanic origin; 10 percent would be Asian and Pacific Islander; and about 1 percent would be American Indian, Eskimo, and Aleut.

Non-Hispanic Whites, the slowest growing group, are likely to contribute less and less to the total population growth in this country. Although non-Hispanic Whites make up almost 75 percent of the total population, they would contribute only 35 percent of the total population growth between 1990 and 2000. This percentage of growth would decrease to 23 percent between 2000 and 2010, and 14 percent from 2010 to 2030. The non-Hispanic White population would contribute nothing to population growth after 2030 because it would be declining in size. According to the middle-series projection, the Black population would increase almost 5 million by 2000, almost 10 million by 2010, and over 20 million by 2030. The Black population would double its present size to 62 million by 2050.

The fastest growing race groups will continue to be the Asian and Pacific Islander population with annual growth rates that may exceed 4 percent during the 1990's. By the turn of the century, the Asian and Pacific Islander population would expand to over 12 million, double its current size by 2010, triple by 2020, and increase to more than 5 times its current size, to 41 million by 2050. Growth of the Hispanic-origin population will probably be a major element of the total population growth.

According to the middle series, the Hispanic-origin population would be the largest growing group. By 2000, the Hispanic-origin population may increase to 31 million, double its 1990 size by 2015, and quadruple its 1990 size by the middle of the next century. In fact, the Hispanic-origin population would contribute 32 percent of the Nation's population growth from 1990 to 2000, 39 percent from 2000 to 2010, 45 percent from 2010 to 2030, and 60 percent from 2030 to 2050.[51]

As a result of this, many races now sit in the seats of justice and leadership. An example is found in Jasper, Texas.

Three white men were indicted Monday on capital murder charges in the death of a black man who was chained to a pickup truck and dragged to his death on a rural East Texas road in early June. One indictment issued by a Jasper County grand jury accuses John William King, 23, of Jasper and Lawrence Russell Brewer, 31, of Sulphur Springs of capital murder. A second indictment by the grand jury names Shawn Allen Berry, 23, of Jasper.... If convicted, the men could face the death penalty in the June 7 slaying of James Byrd Jr.[52]

---

51 National Population Projections, Jennifer Cheeseman Day. Source: U.S. Census Bureau, Population Division. http://csrd.asu.edu/sites/default/files/pdf/Population%20Profile%20of%20the%20United%20States.pdf

52 3 Whites Indicted in Dragging Death of Black Man in Texas, CNN, July 6, 1998. http://www.cnn.com/US/9807/06/dragging.death.02/index.html.

Though far from perfect, America is slowly changing, be it by force or a transition of the minds. Through knowledge, inventions, and technology, the new world is supposed to become better, smarter, and more civilized than the old. The world must stand strong against the horrible disease of racism; our children are depending on us.

CHAPTER 15

RACISM AND THE SOCIETY OF AMERICA

I s the racial divide stemming from weakness, ignorance, or hatred? If weakness is the problem, forward positive progression will be hindered. The weakness of humans is unmistakable and devastating when a person lacks the power to stand for what he or she believes to be right. Weakness is coupled with fear. Even when one knows the right thing to do, pursuit after that right event is oftentimes limited by weakness or fear. Often time's humans fear the consequences of being ostracized, persecuted, or marked for taking a stand. In history, countless evils have prevailed because good people refused to stand for what they knew to be right. Ignorance plagues the hearts of us all in one way or another. It has been said, "Man fears what he doesn't understand." Ignorance plays a major part in racial discord. According to Paul R. Lehman, "Dr Satoshi Kanazawa of the London School of Economics wrote that black women are less attractive and intelligent than women from other racial groups. In so doing, he exposes himself as ignorant, insensitive, and bigoted."[53] Through ignorance, people are empowered to stereotype. Ignorance is very difficult to combat because through ignorance a person is justified in his own mind. Unrestrained hatred destroys its possessor from within. The origin of racial divide begins with hatred. Hatred breeds murder, and the hatred of something is an emotion that few people want but all people have deep within their hearts. There is the hatred of evil, and there is the

---

53 "Kanazawa's Views on Race Shows Ignorance and Bias," by Paul R. Lehman, May 30, 2011. http://americasraceproblem.wordpress.com/?s=Kanazawa%E2%80%99s+views.

hatred of good. The person who hates evil is hated by the person who loves evil. The person who loves evil loves to hate, and we know that most hateful people are resentful and angry inside.

One might define racism as hatred against a person, place, or thing. Hatred is the worst and most widespread disease in the world today. Hatred is devastating because it is a human emotion that is decided by choice. The choice of hatred toward humans is due to superior and inferior attitudes. The world of medicine continues to research fatal diseases. Hatred is a disease that continually exists in humans, with no cure in sight. As it lives in the hearts of humans, it proves to be extremely consuming and aggressive. It spreads like cancer and is found in the hearts of humans. This nation has put up with the evils of hatred for far too long. Violent hate crimes have been the result of our tolerance of this great evil. The adversary has strongly deceived humanity. The adversary of the world is the Devil, and hatred is one of his many tools. Hatred is an extreme attitude against nationality, weight, size, appearance, intelligence, money conditions (rich or poor), and so on. Hatred is an attitude that through education is transferred from one generation to the next. The evils of hatred can be eradicated if each person submits to the will of Jesus Christ, striving to be like Him. The world needs to get to know the King of kings and Creator of the universe. God is fair and just and shows no partiality. Jesus taught us the principle of the Golden Rule: "Do unto others as you would that they do unto you" (Matt. 7:12). That rule in itself demolishes the adversary of good.

Why is hatred so prevalent in this racial divide? Here are eight possible answers for the world to consider. First, hatred stems from ignorance. Second, the world possesses a lack of understanding and is very opinionated. Third, different cultures bring undesired challenges. Fourth, hatred is coupled together with envy. Envy was the reason stated by Pilate that Jesus was delivered over to death. The fifth reason is jealousy. Jealous hearts are a tremendously destructive force. Sixth is self-condemnation. People's hearts are condemned daily by their guilty consciences. The seventh is selfishness. Selfish minds will do just about anything and go along with whatever they have to in order to get ahead in life. Finally, a low self-esteem demands that people follow instead of lead.

Racism is a security issue. Individuals with racist minds are usually very insecure. They are unsure of themselves and attempt to belittle others. Belittling others in their mind increases their worth or value.

However, to bring one person down to another's level does not increase self-worth. Racism is rooted in the complete ignorance of others. Thoughtlessness is the measuring rod of racism. How is it possible to hate someone whom a person has never met? The idea itself is ludicrous.

Racial intolerance regarding America's diverse nationalities is strong. The United States of America does not belong to one race of people. We must remember how America became the land of opportunity.

> American history began with waves of immigrants, bringing their own cultures and traditions to a vast new country. There is no other place in the world with such a diverse population. This diversity that makes America what it is and, at the same time, creates the challenges it faces ... Strictly speaking, the only indigenous Americans are the American Indians who were living here long before the first waves of settlers came over from Europe. When Christopher Columbus discovered America in 1492, he called these natives "Indians" because he thought he had discovered a western route to India. Today the trend is toward multiculturalism, not assimilation. The old "melting pot" metaphor is giving way to new metaphors such as "salad bowl" and "mosaic," mixtures of various ingredients that keep their individual characteristics. Immigrant populations within the United States are not being blended together in one "pot," but rather they are transforming American Society into a truly multicultural mosaic. The American mosaic is one of different cultures and regional identities, each with unique characteristics and flavors. Americans often think of themselves not only as coming from a particular ethnic heritage, but also of being part of a geographical region. Understanding these regional characteristics and flavors is an excellent way to get to know Americans.[54]

The racial issues of intolerance must be solved.

---

54 Understanding American Culture: From Melting Pot to Salad Bowl," by Joyce Millet, 2000. http://www.culturalsavvy.com/understanding_american_culture.htm

CHAPTER 16

RACISM AND RELIGION IN AMERICA

It is time for the church to pray diligently for a solution to the issues of hate. God is the world's only answer. God is humanity's true and lasting solution. Our souls have become weakened from the absence of obedience to God and from the absence of an active prayer life. True unadulterated Christianity is our only solution. Jesus Christ can resolve racism as He resolves every other attitude that is opposed to righteousness.

Humans must choose not to allow resentment, pride, and animosity to fester in their hearts. God has given humankind a free will. The freedom to choose requires a desire to execute a plan. Booker T. Washington said, "I will permit no man to narrow and degrade my soul by making me hate him." Humanity must forgive the issues of the past. Issues of the past can continue to remain deep within the hearts, or people can choose to turn these issues over to the Lord. Humanity has an important decision to make. Is there a cure for hatred? Yes! There is a cure for hatred. That cure is love. The cycle of hatred in this world can end if the right choices are made. Jesus says to "love your enemies and to pray for them that persecute you" (Matt. 5:44).

Racism is a shameful mark on Christianity. Sadly, racism in some churches is still an issue to this day. There are African American churches and Caucasian churches. Some Christians have a strong desire to assemble with their own race to protect the purity of their race and the chasm of segregation. God sees one race, the human race. Christians need to become like God and less like self. It is sad to say that many of America's churches still struggle with issues of race. Do

Christians see it? If not, why not? Christians must open their eyes to the feelings of others. Racial discrimination stems from deep within the human heart. It is deep within the heart because of the emotional trauma inflicted by our past. It is deep within the heart because of societal indoctrination. This racial hatred among religious people even carries over to a hatred of the Jewish nation. Have racist religious people forgotten that Jesus Christ was a Jew? Do these religious people hate Jesus too? Hatred trickles down from one generation to another, and unfortunately, there is no end in sight.

John the beloved Apostle of God understood the message of love. He declares to his readers that everything in life must revolve around love. He identifies that the love problem is people loving people. The depth of the problem is people loving God. People look at other people in different ways, instead of seeing them as they see themselves. People look at people and prejudge them. Prejudiced eyes are constantly looking through a clouded window. They look out and see flaws, not realizing that the flaws exist because the windows of their hearts are dirty. Though humans look different, there is not one superior to another. The battle of race exists not just with black and white, but also viewing skin complexions as being too dark or too light. Amazingly, some African Americans hate African Americans, and some Caucasians hate Caucasians. Some hate their own ethnicity. These people are in self-denial, possessing a low self-esteem. The proof of their low self-esteem is found in their hating their own ethnicity, which is the equivalent of hating themselves. This attitude not only comes from the refusal to look deep into the recesses of their own hearts, but also from indoctrination. Parents, family, the media, and friends teach this indoctrination. The indoctrination of racism is evil and terroristic.

In the first book of John, chapter four, verse twenty, John says, "If someone says, 'I love God,' and hates his brother, he is a liar; for the one who does not love his brother whom he has seen, cannot love God whom he has not seen." How can people say that they love God and hate their brother? The world is full of liars and hypocrites. God says that it is impossible to love Him if we cannot love one another. The beloved Apostle Paul tells each Christian the truth about what he or she is supposed to see in a fellow Christian. He says, in second Corinthians, chapter five, verse sixteen, "Therefore from now on we recognize no man according to the flesh; even though we have known

Christ according to the flesh, yet now we know Him thus no longer." If one cannot look into the eyes of his or her fellow human and see the creation of God, that person's mind is confused.

All peoples added to the body of Christ are Christians. How could one who is made a Christian by way of a gift feel superior to another? Salvation is a free gift for all who will but receive it. A loving Savior frees baptized believers from a life of sin. Through baptism, all peoples become one in Christ Jesus. Christians must love each other regardless of gender, ethnicity, geographical location, or culture. Christians must take the lead in ending the racial conflict. God calls His followers to lead by example. Christians are called to follow Jesus and to be lights to a dark, cold, perverse, and dying world. Christians must love each other for the following reasons: First, they are born into the same adopted family. Second, each person is saved by the same needed grace. Third, Christians are walking by the same faith in Christ Jesus. Fourth, there is only one God, and Christians share a common belief in that same God. Fifth, godly people walk by the same fruits of the spirit and are dependent on the dynamic mercy of God. Sixth, Christians must love each other because of their common struggles against sin.

All Christians have a familiar enemy and strong adversary. Together, all Christians should be fighting against the forces of evil. Paul says, "For our struggle is not against flesh and blood, but against the rulers, against the powers, against the world forces of this darkness, against the spiritual forces of wickedness in the heavenly places" (Eph. 6:12). The spiritual battle is not against our fellow humans; it is against the forces of evil in this spirit world. John tells his readers that loving their fellow humans is a commandment from God. He says, "And this commandment we have from Him, that the one who loves God should love his brother also" (1 John 4:21). Christians must love one another and their enemies as well. "Ye have heard that it was said, Thou shalt love thy neighbor, and hate thine enemy: but I say unto you, love your enemies, and pray for them that persecute you" (Matt. 5:43–44).

Most people have told common racial jokes that are both offensive and degrading. The same human being that God commands all to love has been shattered and crushed from the tongues of another. The tongue used in an evil way has caused Christian brothers and sisters emotional pain. Some have been insulted, which creates strong tension and friction during their worship opportunities. Instead of unity, there is division, dissatisfaction, disgust, and discord. Christians must use their words with skill and godliness. Jesus says in Matthew 12:36—37, "And I say to you, that every careless word that men shall speak, they shall render account for it in the Day of Judgment. For by your words, you shall be justified, and by your word you shall be condemned." Saints must learn to choose their words very carefully. Careless words have been the downfall of many friendships. If church members find it difficult to get along, how can they ever expect the world to share in the bond of unity?

Words spoken are the thoughts expressed from a person's mind. Jesus explains this concept to the world in Mark 7:18–23 saying:

> And he saith unto them, Are ye so without understanding also? Perceive ye not, that whatsoever from without goeth into the man, it cannot defile him; because it goeth not into his heart, but into his belly, and goeth out into the draught? This He said, making all meats clean. And he said, that which proceeded out of the man that defiled the man. For from within, out of the heart of men, evil thoughts proceed, fornications, thefts, murders, adulteries, covetings, wickednesses, deceit, lasciviousness, an evil eye, railing, pride, foolishness: all these evil things proceed from within, and defile the man.

The evil thoughts from within eventually become evident by the tongues of humans. Hence, the expression, "Today he showed his true colors."

Some ask, "Am I a racist?" An important fact to remember is that discrimination is not limited to people. To dislike an object, cause, decree, or disease with an objective legitimate reason is not always wrong or bad. If one dislikes certain foods, music, or lifestyles, that is a matter of one's own personal choice, and that choice must be respected by others. The question is not "Am I a racist?" The question is: "What have I done to demonstrate the attitude and spirit of racism? Do I have my thoughts, actions, and emotions under control?"

Through racism, many Christians have become stumbling blocks to the world and are condemned by God. God does not want anyone to be an obstacle to another. Please understand that when churches practice racial division, the feeling of betrayal digs deep into the core of the offended parties' minds. Jesus says in Luke 17:1–2, "And he said unto his disciples, It is impossible but that occasions of stumbling should come; but woe unto him, through whom they come! It were well for him if a millstone were hanged about his neck, and he were thrown into the sea, rather than that he should cause one of these little ones to stumble." Satan uses this division and these obstacles as tools to destroy the souls of humanity. Peter's hypocrisy could have been tremendously damaging if the Apostle Paul had remained silent.

> But when Cephas came to Antioch, I resisted him to the face, because he stood condemned. For before that certain came from James, he ate with the Gentiles; but when they came, he drew back and separated himself, fearing them that were of the circumcision. And the rest of the Jews dissembled likewise with him; insomuch that even Barnabas was carried away with their dissimulation. But when I saw that they walked not uprightly according to the truth of the gospel, I said unto Cephas before *them* all, If thou, being a Jew, livest as do the Gentiles, and not as do the Jews, how compellest thou the Gentiles to live as do the Jews? (Gal 2:11).

The Jews believed that they were a superior race over the Gentiles. They thought that they were a far better people than the rest. Racism is pride in action. The Jews believed that they were superior because they had a special relationship with God. Yet the Bible says emphatically that, "God so loved the world" (John 3:16). Paul shows the Jews their misunderstanding and confusion on race issues in Romans chapters one through three. There, he declared that the Gentiles to their shame were committing many sins. As the Jewish nation sided with Paul on this issue, Paul informs the Jews that they are no better because they are guilty of the same. The reality is that, "All have sinned and come short of the glory of God" (Rom. 3:23).

Humanity needs to be mature, spiritually minded, and honest enough to admit that there are good and bad people in every race. There is not one race of people who are all bad; neither is there one race of people who are all good. No one individual does good all of the time. Each human has his or her faults. Humanity must be wise

101

enough to know that it is unsound to condemn or hate an entire race of people just because of the actions of one individual member of that particular race. Think for just a moment. It is impossible to get perfect service from every grocery store, restaurant, or fast-food chain. Very few people, even with good reason, will hate an entire chain of companies just because they received bad service at one place. When bad service is experienced at one place, responsible adults simply choose to go to another or return to the same location at another time of the day. It is shameful seeing some of the things that humans have done to an entire race simply because of the actions of one individual. In the book of Esther, Haman hated Mordecai, and his hatred drove him to attempt the complete destruction and annihilation of a nation. One person's inadequacies or weaknesses do not condemn, condone, or tear down an entire race of people.

Ezekiel 18:4 teaches, "The soul that sins will die." God does not hold one person accountable for another's sins. As Jesus says, "For the Son of man shall come in the glory of his Father with his angels; and then shall he render unto every man according to his deeds" (Matt. 16:27). As our law demands, a person is innocent until proven guilty. No person is accountable for what others do; rather, each person is accountable for what he or she does. How long will good people be condemned and hated along with an entire race simply because of the actions of one person within that particular race?

All are made in the image of God. As the Holy Scriptures teach, we are physically and spiritually united together as one. Take a moment to consider Scriptures from the Word of God.

> And God said, "Let us make man in our image, after our likeness: and let them have dominion over the fish of the sea, and over the birds of the heavens, and over the cattle, and over all the earth, and over every creeping thing that creepeth upon the earth (Gen. 1:26).

> And the man called his wife's name Eve; because she was the mother of all living (Gen. 3:20).

> The God that made the world and all things therein, He, being Lord of heaven and earth, dwelleth not in temples made with hands; neither is he served by

men's hands, as though he needed anything, seeing he himself giveth to all life, and breath, and all things; and he made of one every nation of men to dwell on all the face of the earth, having determined their appointed seasons, and the bounds of their habitation; that they should seek God, if haply they might feel after him and find him, though he is not far from each one of us: for in him we live, and move, and have our being; as certain even of your own poets have said, For we are also his offspring (Acts 17:24–28).

But ye are an elect race, a royal priesthood, a holy nation, a people for God's own possession, that ye may show forth the excellencies of him who called you out of darkness into his marvellous light: who in time past were no people, but now are the people of God: who had not obtained mercy, but now have obtained mercy (1 Peter 2:9–10).

There can be neither Jew nor Greek, there can be neither bond nor free, there can be no male and female; for ye all are one man in Christ Jesus. And if ye are Christ's, then are ye Abraham's seed, heirs according to promise (Gal. 3:28–29).

And now in Christ Jesus our Lord, His body of believers, the church, is spiritually united as one. As Jesus prayed, "Neither for these only do I pray, but for them also that believe on me through their word; that they may all be one; even as thou, Father, *art* in me, and I in thee, that they also may be in us: that the world may believe that thou didst send me" (John 17:20–21). Thank God for His magnificent gift of love.

Will humanity ever forgive the mistakes and sins of the past? Humankind cannot move forward until individuals forgive as the Lord has commanded. The teachings and parables of Jesus illustrate forgiveness repeatedly. God mandates forgiveness! Love is the only way; all must learn tolerance and equality. "He that loveth not knoweth not God; for God is love. Herein was the love of God manifested in us, that God hath sent his only begotten Son into the world that we might live through him. Herein is love, not that we loved God, but that he loved us, and sent his Son to be the propitiation for our sins. Beloved, if God so loved us, we also ought to love one another" (1 John 4:8–11). Remember the words of Jesus, who says, "The first is, Hear, O Israel; The Lord our God, the Lord is one: and thou shalt love the Lord thy God with all thy heart, and with all thy soul, and with all thy mind, and with all thy strength. The second is this, Thou shalt love thy neighbor as thyself. There is none other commandment greater than these" (Mark 12:29–31). Humanity must commit and submit to the teachings of Jesus Christ, abiding by the Golden Rule. "All things therefore whatsoever ye would that men should do unto you, even so do ye also unto them ..." (Matt. 7:12). "Be not deceived; God is not mocked: for whatsoever a man soweth, that shall he also reap" (Gal. 6:7).

The hearts of humanity must go through a complete transformation, becoming spiritually minded and becoming more like God every day. "I beseech you therefore, brethren, by the mercies of God, to present your bodies a living sacrifice, holy, acceptable to God, which is your spiritual service. And be not fashioned according to this world: but be ye transformed by the renewing of your mind, and ye may prove what is the good and acceptable and perfect will of God" (Rom. 12:1–2). The appeal from God is that a complete transformation of the mind will occur.

CHAPTER 17

THE HOPE OF A TRANSITION IN THE WORLD TODAY

One of the greatest speeches during the civil rights era was given by Dr. Martin Luther King.

> I have a dream that one day every valley shall be exalted, every hill and mountain shall be made low, the rough places will be made plain, and the crooked places will be made straight, and the glory of the Lord shall be revealed, and all flesh shall see it together. This is our hope. This is the faith that I go back to the South with. With this faith we will be able to hew out of the mountain of despair a stone of hope. With this faith we will be able to transform the jangling discords of our nation into a beautiful symphony of brotherhood.[55]

It is all about making the right choices and doing the right things. The decisions that are made today will tremendously affect our children's future. Good, moral, and responsible decisions by independent thinkers must be made that will affect the present and the future generations for the ultimate good of humanity. Perhaps with the help of God, this dream will become a reality. Prayerfully this dream can be realized over the entire world. Yet not this dream alone but other dreams that seek equality among all human beings. Every human

---

55   The Huffington Post, January 17, 2011, http://www.huffingtonpost.com/2011/01/17/i-have-a-dream-speech-text_n_809993.html.

being deserves to be treated in a Nondiscriminatory and humane way because we have all been created equal and in the image of God.

One thing remains: the prayer that all of humankind will submit to the will of God and be saved. What does the Bible teach regarding how one is saved? First, one must hear the Word of God, as stated in Romans 10:17, "So belief cometh of hearing, and hearing by the word of Christ." Second, the hearer must believe the message of the Gospel. Jesus says, "I said therefore unto you, that ye shall die in your sins: for except ye believe that I am *he*, ye shall die in your sins" (John 8:24). Third, the believer must repent or have godly sorrow in his or her heart. Acts 17:30 contrasts the days of old with today. It says, "The times of ignorance therefore God overlooked; but now he commandeth men that they should all everywhere repent." Fourth, a confession must be made. The confession is that Jesus Christ is the Son of the living God. Jesus tells us in Matthew 10:32–33: "Every one therefore who shall confess me before men, him will I also confess before my Father who is in heaven. But whosoever shall deny me before men, him will I also deny before my Father who is in heaven." Fifth, all of humankind has been found guilty of sin and must have these sins washed away. Biblically speaking, baptism is what washes a sinner clean. In 1 Peter chapter 3, verse 21, it says: "which also after a true likeness doth now save you, *even* baptism, not the putting away of the filth of the flesh, but the interrogation of a good conscience toward God, through the resurrection of Jesus Christ." (Also see Acts 22:16.) Finally, one must walk with the Lord until the day that God calls him or her home. All Christians are to be faithful to God until death, as seen in Revelations 2:10, which states: "Fear not the things which thou art about to suffer: behold, the devil is about to cast some of you into prison, that ye may be tried; and ye shall have tribulation ten days. Be thou faithful unto death, and I will give thee the crown of life."

GLOSSARY

CIVIL RIGHTS

A civil right is an enforceable right or privilege, which if interfered with by another gives rise to an action for injury. Examples of civil rights are freedom of speech, press, and assembly; the right to vote; freedom from involuntary servitude; and the right to equality in public places. Discrimination occurs when the civil rights of an individual are denied or interfered with because of their membership in a particular group or class. Various jurisdictions have enacted statutes to prevent discrimination based on a person's race, sex, religion, age, previous condition of servitude, physical limitation, national origin, and in some instances sexual orientation.

The most important expansions of civil rights in the United States occurred as a result of the enactment of the Thirteenth and Fourteenth Amendments of the U.S. Constitution. The Thirteenth Amendment abolished slavery throughout the United States. *See* U.S. Const. amend. XIII. In response to the Thirteenth Amendment, various states enacted "black codes" that were intended to limit the civil rights of the newly free slaves. In 1868 the Fourteenth Amendment countered these "black codes" by stating that no state "shall make or enforce any law which shall abridge the privileges or immunities of the citizens of the United States … [or] deprive any person of life, liberty, or property without due process of law, [or] deny to any person within its jurisdiction the equal protection of the laws." *See* U.S. Const. amend. XIV. Section Five of the Fourteenth Amendment gave Congress the power by section five of the Fourteenth Amendment to pass any laws needed to enforce the Amendment.

During the reconstruction era that followed, Congress enacted numerous civil rights statutes. Many of these are still in force today and protect individuals from discrimination and from the deprivation of their civil rights. Section 1981 of Title 42 (Equal Rights Under the Law) protects individuals from discrimination based on race in making and enforcing contracts, participating in lawsuits, and giving evidence. *See* 42 U.S.C. § 1981.[56]

COCAINE

"Cocaine is usually distributed as a white, crystalline powder. Cocaine is often diluted ("cut") with a variety of substances, the most common of which are sugars and local anesthetics. It is "cut" to stretch the amount of the product and increase profits for dealers. In contrast, cocaine base (crack) looks like small, irregularly shaped chunks (or "rocks") of a whitish solid."[57]

CRACK

Crack is cocaine in a solid form. It is made by dissolving two parts of cocaine and 1 part of water, and adding baking soda to it, which makes it turn into a solid. The mixed part is then cooked over an open flame. After a few minutes, it turns into what is known as a "rock."

CRACK HOUSE

A crack house is a building, usually without electricity or gas and illuminated by a candle, being occupied by drug addicts. The building is usually filthy and void of furniture. Crack addicts spend most of their time there. Some of the regulars are employed by the drug dealer, and the employees are paid pennies in drugs. It is an open market, with endless drug dealers, users, and drugs.

CREW

A crew is a type of small gang. Many gangs have been formed from crews. A crew begins as a close-knit group dealing in petty crime,

---

56 Cornell University Law School,
    Legal Information Institute
    Civil Rights
    August 19, 2010, 5:12 pm
    http://www.law.cornell.edu/wex/Civil_rights

57 US Department of Justice, 950 Pennsylvania Avenue, NW, Washington, DC
    20530-0001. Drug Fact Sheet-Cocaine
    Drug Enforcement Administration
    http://www.justice.gov/dea/druginfo/drug_data_sheets/Cocaine.pdf

which later expands in size and criminal activity, ultimately evolving into a gang.

DISGUISED

Prejudice is disguised in churches because the church preaches one God and one people but acts contrary to its preaching. Churches were leaders of hate but claimed to be followers of God. They preached unity but practiced segregation. They demanded to be heard but would not speak up. America disguises stereotypes through affirmative action. Stereotyping is disguised because, though it is engrained in the heart, it is unspoken.

DRUG ENFORCEMENT ADMINISTRATION (DEA)

"The Drug Enforcement Administration was created by President Richard Nixon through an Executive Order in July 1973 in order to establish a single unified command to combat 'an all-out global war on the drug menace."[58]

GANG

Gangs are defined in many ways, and most definitions have similar components. One common definition of a gang is a group of three or more individuals who engage in criminal activity and identify themselves with a common name or sign.

"Once found principally in large cities, violent street gangs now affect public safety, community image, and quality of life in communities of all sizes in urban, suburban, and rural areas. No region of the United States is untouched by gangs. Gangs affect society at all levels, causing heightened fears for safety, violence, and economic costs" (*2005 National Gang Threat Assessment*, National Alliance of Gang Investigators Associations, 2005).[59]

"Some 20,000 violent street gangs, motorcycle gangs, and prison gangs with nearly one million members are criminally active in the U.S.

---

58 US Department of Justice, 950 Pennsylvania Avenue, NW, Washington, DC 20530-0001.
Drug Enforcement Administration
http://www.justice.gov/dea/about/history.shtml.

59 National Criminal Justice Reference Service, Administered by the Office of Justice Programs, US Department of Justice. https://www.ncjrs.gov/spotlight/gangs/summary.html.

today. Many are sophisticated and well organized; all use violence to control neighborhoods and boost their illegal money-making activities, which include robbery, drug and gun trafficking, fraud, extortion, and prostitution rings."[60]

Members of gangs are also often referred to as "gangbangers."

GANGSTA

The word *gangsta* is simply a spinoff from the word *gangster*. A gangsta is a street soldier who is a protector of his or her community against all threats foreign or domestic. He or she is usually involved in gangs, gang violence, drug trafficking, and other types of criminal activity.

Gangstas are also referred to as soldiers. Soldiers in the hood and urban areas are protectors of the streets.

GHETTO

A ghetto is a place created by racial segregation. Being the recipients of inequality and subject to the "Jim Crow" laws, blacks needed a place to go. Blacks were involved in the racially charged struggle against equality. With low incomes and the destructive forces of segregation, blacks were limited in their choices of where to live. These predominantly black and Hispanic neighborhoods became known as ghettos, or "the projects."

These impoverished areas still exist, carrying with them the name from the past. Now government assistance and programs keep these rundown, bug-infested dwelling places from being condemned.

The term *ghetto* also refers to the image or appearance of individuals and the way that a person carries himself or herself, his or her mentality, and the way that he or she acts or dresses.

GRAFFITI

Graffiti is a type of artwork that generally is against the law because of its location. Found on walls, abandoned property, and the streets in urban neighborhoods, graffiti is used to mark territory, identify gangs, and warn neighborhoods of gang or police activity and many additional things.

---

60 FBI Headquarters, 935 Pennsylvania Avenue, NW, Washington, DC 20535-0001, (202) 324-3000. http://www.fbi.gov/about-us/investigate/vc_majorthefts/gangs/gangs.

In modern times, paint, particularly spray paint, and marker pens have become the most commonly used graffiti materials. In most countries, marking or painting property without the property owner's consent is considered defacement and vandalism, which is a punishable crime. Graffiti may also express underlying social and political messages and a whole genre of artistic expression is based upon spray paint graffiti styles. Within hip hop culture, graffiti has evolved alongside hip hop music, b-boying, and other elements. Unrelated to hip-hop graffiti, gangs use their own form of graffiti to mark territory or to serve as an indicator of gang-related activities.[61]

HOOD

The hood is a shortened version for neighborhood. The hood, simply stated, is where a person lives. The hood most generally refers to a ghetto or the projects.

The hood is a place filled with people in poverty and even deep poverty. Many of its residents are on welfare and food stamps. Section 8 housing is the norm. The hood is a place filled with low income houses or many high-rise apartments. It then is comprised of families with middle class or low income and those within the welfare system. It is a place usually filled with crime and criminals and is a very dangerous place to live.

The word can also refer to someone who is from the ghetto or acts as if he or she is from the ghetto.

HOODLUM

Hoodlum, hooligan are names given to a person who disregards the laws of the land. These are people who have a history of destruction and violence. You can find them hanging out on street corners in gangs, clubs, or bars.

INNER CITY

Inner city has a dual connotation. It can refer to a location or a situation. Thus, the phrase *inner city* is another mind-set. Many inner-city children do not live inside of the ghettos or hoods. In fact, some inner-city children live in country areas. They can live outside

---

61 Wikipedia. http://en.wikipedia.org/wiki/Graffiti, last modified on 9 September 2011 at 22:55.

of the hood but hang out with people from the hood. Perhaps they attend the same schools, are on the same athletic teams, or are simply friends. Inner-city children are not just those living in a certain location deprived of help, but also a disadvantaged people. Poverty extends outside of the ghetto; these youths living outside of the inner-city community are accepted as if they live next door. One might also use phrases such as *urban society* or *metropolitan area.*

KIX

A slang term used to represent a pair of shoes.

LATCHKEY CHILD

The baby boomers were the generation largely responsible for introducing the lifestyle of latchkey children. A latchkey child is a child who was often at home alone, primarily coming home to an empty house from school or play. Parents of these children were at work as they enjoyed a booming economy. During this era, child-care centers began to thrive.

NATIONAL ASSOCIATION FOR THE ADVANCEMENT OF COLORED PEOPLE (NAACP)

Founded Feb. 12, 1909, the NAACP is the nation's oldest, largest and most widely recognized grassroots-based civil rights organization. Its more than half-million members and supporters throughout the United States and the world are the premier advocates for civil rights in their communities, campaigning for equal opportunity and conducting voter mobilization …

The NAACP's principal objective is to ensure the political, educational, social and economic equality of minority group citizens of United States and eliminate race prejudice. The NAACP seeks to remove all barriers of racial discrimination through the democratic processes.[62]

SECTION 8

"Section 8 of the United States Housing Act of 1937 (often simply known as Section 8), as repeatedly amended, authorizes the payment of rental housing assistance to private landlords on behalf of

---

62 National Association for the Advancement of Colored People, 4805 Mt. Hope Drive, Baltimore MD 21215, Local: (410) 580-5777, Toll-Free: (877) NAACP-98. © 2009–2011. http://www.naacp.org/pages/naacp-history.

approximately 3.1 million low-income households. It operates through several programs, the largest of which, the Housing Choice Voucher program, pays a large portion of the rents and utilities of about 2.1 million households."[63]

"The housing choice voucher program is the federal government's major program for assisting very low-income families, the elderly, and the disabled to afford decent, safe, and sanitary housing in the private market ..."[64]

SELLOUT

A "sellout" is a person who changes in a positive or negative direction. It carries the perception that one has forgotten his or her roots. A sellout is one who changes his or her view and loyalty in any way, which includes lifestyle, music, popularity, and finance.

STEREOTYPES

Stereotypes are destroying the world because they have led to many false conclusions. From a logical perspective, whenever the premises are false, the conclusion is false. False conclusions prove to be destructive. False conclusions cloud and clutter the minds of humanity. A preconceived idea may be true or false. Morals and principles of life hinge on these ideas. If the idea is false, then the moral will become immoral. Stereotypes lead us to lies, injustice, and profiling. They stand in the way of progress.

THUG

Thug is not a word that means ignorant. Some thugs are very intelligent academically, but most are simply streetwise. Being a thug is a mind-set. It stems from within a person who struggles yet strives to overcome in some way. It is the mind-set of refusal. Thugs refuse to allow others to walk all over them, so they retaliate. A thug's retaliation can be through art, poetry, music, academics, and many other ways. The idea behind the word *thug* is that the thug is a product of a society that he or she strives either to get out of or to dominate.

---

63 Wikipedia. http://en.wikipedia.org/wiki/Section_8_(housing), last modified on 6 September 2011 at 13:24.

64 Wikipedia. http://portal.hud.gov/hudportal/HUD?src=/topics/housing_choice_voucher_program_section_8.

A thug can be a gang leader who uses wise strategies to run his large organizations. Thugs are ruthless individuals and leaders. The term "thuggin" demonstrates the actions of the mind-set (what he or she does).

An example is shown through Jay Z, who proclaimed that he was "hood forever," which means once a thug, always a thug by choice. The mind-set of a thug is to strive continually for excellence in whatever area or field with which he or she finds himself or herself involved. Within this person remain the wounds (physical, spiritual and emotional), weaknesses and strengths from his or her past. Even when he or she finds success, he or she may still possess some of his or her old ways.

WANNABE

A wannabe is an individual who is not in a gang but perhaps wants to be. They do many vicious, grotesque, and gory crimes to enter into a gang and to gain a name or quick reputation.

We can also define wannabes as people who listen to and appreciate the art of rap music; attempting to relate to the lyrics, they pretend to be hardcore or mimic what they see in movies or hear in the songs from the hood.

WELFARE

Federally funded and governed US welfare began in the 1930's during the Great Depression. The US government responded to the overwhelming number of families and individuals in need of aid by creating a welfare program that would give assistance to those who had little or no income.

Most states offer basic aid such as health care, food stamps, child care assistance, unemployment, cash aid, and housing assistance.[65]

WINGS

People in the wings are those who follow a crowd but have no real commitment to the cause or rebellion; they do not hold to its values.

---

65   WelfareInfo.org. Welfare Information, © 2011 http://www.welfareinfo.org/.

www.ingramcontent.com/pod-product-compliance
Lightning Source LLC
Chambersburg PA
CBHW020538290526
45786CB00002B/941